VERGIL
for
BEGINNERS

A Dual Approach
to Early Vergil Study

By
ROSE WILLIAMS

Bolchazy-Carducci Publishers, Inc.
Wauconda, Illinois USA

MW00365754

General Editor
Vicki Wine

Contributing Editor
LeaAnn A. Osburn

Cover Design & Typography
Adam Phillip Velez

Cover & Interior Illustrations
James Hillyer Estes

Vergil for Beginners
A Dual Approach to Early Vergil Study

Rose Williams

Bolchazy-Carducci Publishers, Inc.
1000 Brown Street
Wauconda, IL 60084 USA
www.bolchazy.com

Printed in the United States of America
2006
by United Graphics

ISBN-13: 978-0-86516-628-8
ISBN-10: 0-86516-628-5

Library of Congress Cataloging-in-Publication Data

Williams, Rose, 1937-
Vergil for beginners : a dual approach to early Vergil study / by Rose Williams.
p. cm.
ISBN-13: 978-0-86516-628-8 (pbk. : alk. paper)
ISBN-10: 0-86516-628-5 (pbk. : alk. paper)
1. Latin language--Readers--Poetry. 2. Virgil. Aeneis. 3. Latin poetry--History
and criticism. I. Title.

PA6801.A3W55 2006
478.6'421--dc22

2006002158

CONTENTS

ILLUSTRATIONS

PREFACE

This book is intended as a reading supplement to be used near the end of students' most basic Latin study. While any of several approaches, reading or grammar/translation or some mixture of the two, ideally will help the students to develop the ability to handle Latin literature as they reach an advanced level, introductory Latin is taught by widely varying methods, stressing different skills at different points. Thus there are two approaches to this book, which may be used separately, used alternately, or mixed together, as the needs of the individual classes dictate.

APPROACH I:
(for non-traditional or reading-based classes)

1. Read the Introduction and discuss the importance of the *Aeneid* and the summary of Vergil's life; then read and discuss the first two paragraphs of the *Aeneid* summary (in Section I).

2. Read through and practice orally Section III: Reading Latin Poetry.

3. Read Scene I of *The Many Worlds of Aeneas*.

4. Read through the Selection 1 Latin passage just for the sound. (This passage has already been experienced in the Reading Latin Poetry section.)

5. Go through the Latin-to-Latin Vocabulary and Vocabulary Aids, if desired.

   OR

   Do the Carpe Grammaticam exercises for Selection 1, using the Word Bank; then go to the Latin-to-Latin Vocabulary and Vocabulary Aids for Selection 1.

6. Discuss what the passage says in general.

   OR

   Translate the passage. (When approaching the Latin passage, teachers might photocopy the Latin passage, then have the students, using the photocopies, take colored markers and, making suggestions as a group and acting as a group, mark all accusatives with purple, all nominatives with red, all verbs with blue. Then, again taking suggestions as a group and acting as a group with some teacher input, students may write a small "1" above each word that goes to make up the first subject, a small "2" over each word that goes to make up the first direct object, and so forth. The photocopies may then be used as a guide for the passage.)

7. Answer the comprehension and discussion questions individually or as a group.

Approach II:
(for traditional or grammar/translation-based classes)

1. Read the Introduction and discuss the importance of the *Aeneid* and the summary of Vergil's life; then read and discuss the first two paragraphs of the *Aeneid* summary (in Section I).

2. Read the play and the Latin Poetry section, if desired.

3. Do the Carpe Grammaticam exercises for Selection 1, using the Word Bank.

4. Go through the Latin-to-Latin Vocabulary and the Vocabulary Aids for Selection 1.

5. Translate the selection.

6. Answer the comprehension and discussion questions.

Selections for Comprehension
This book features six selections from Books I, II, IV, and VI of the *Aeneid*, chosen to highlight the major points of the story.

Selection 1: Juno visits Aeolus and asks him to create a storm to shipwreck Aeneas and his crew.

Selection 2: Aeneas makes provision for his shipwrecked men.

Selection 3: Aeneas tells at the banquet about the signs from the gods and his departure from Troy.

Selection 4: Dido suffers from love for Aeneas.

Selection 5: Aeneas visits Anchises in Elysium.

Selection 6: Anchises predicts Rome's greatness.

Students who know some Latin should have a chance to experience this outstanding work in the original. In addition to acquainting the students with the greatest work of Latin literature, this book hopes to serve these other purposes:

- to encourage Latin to Latin comprehension,

- to expand and review student vocabulary,

- to provide grammar review in a literary context.

LATIN-TO-LATIN VOCABULARY

One good study approach is comparing Vergil's extensive vocabulary with more general words the students probably know. This enables the readers to gain a general idea of the meaning of the target selection before they employ the usual approaches to a passage of Latin. The Latin-to-Latin vocabulary selections are chosen for several reasons; some are used because they are common Latin words studied by most beginning students; some because they are very similar in appearance to the general meaning sought; some because they have already been used in the text; some because they throw light on an unusual word use by Vergil. Sometimes Vergil uses a less familiar word because it fits his meter better, or because he wants to portray a shade of meaning. Students can benefit by comparing his word to other words they know to establish a general idea of the selected passage. Then, with vocabulary aids and grammar review exercises, they can approach the passage again to explore its more subtle and exact wording.

INTRODUCTION

Vergil's *Aeneid* is a very long poem of the type called epic. These poems often told about heroes who shaped or changed the history of their country and in this way affected the lives of many people. The *Aeneid* is one of the very greatest of these epics, and since the time when it was written it has had a great influence on literature and on the world's ideas about the Romans. People through the ages have praised it, studied it, and loved it. This is because Vergil had a very special talent for making his audience understand, appreciate, and learn from people who had already been dead a thousand years when he was writing. He helps us all to see that the situations these people faced recur in every human generation and have meaning for us today.

DEITIES

One of the most difficult things readers new to Latin must learn to understand is the position of deities in the ancient classical world, which has very little to do with the concept of deity usually accepted today. There were many ancient deities forming a whole society, like a race of people. Some were related to each other, and some were much more powerful than others. A few were very powerful indeed, and could bring prosperity or destruction to humankind as they chose. Nearly all of them could be kind or cruel, and their decisions could be made on the spur of the moment, depending on whether they had been pleased by an offering or annoyed by some slight. These gods were, with a few exceptions, like humans, only much more bright and beautiful, proud and jealous of their position and their prestige. Standing in the shadows behind them were the Fates, three mysterious women who spun the thread of life, wove its tapestry, and cut the thread when life was done. The Fates were not moved by emotions or by prayers, and neither gods nor men, however much they tried, could change what the Fates decreed. Vergil uses these giant figures as the backdrop for the struggles of humankind that are often so hard for us to understand. He shows us characters who keep trying to accomplish what they set out to do, regardless of the obstacles suddenly placed in their path. Some of his people succeed and triumph; some fail and perish miserably, just as people do today.

VERGIL'S STYLE

Since one of the most outstanding features of Vergil's monumental work is its simplicity, a beginning reader with very little understanding of Latin's complexity needs only a good source of vocabulary words to enjoy some of the most memorable scenes and characters from the *Aeneid.*

PUBLIUS VERGILIUS MARO, 70 BCE–19 BCE

Vergil, who is considered Rome's greatest epic poet and one of the greatest of world literature, was born near Mantua in northern Italy, and educated at Cremona, Mediolanum, and Rome. By 37 BCE he had published the ten *Eclogues (Bucolics),* poems about shepherds and country life. The poems were very popular, and they brought Vergil to the attention of Maecenas, a rich man who loved literature and often provided living expenses for writers. Maecenas was a very good friend of the Emperor Augustus, who also liked literature and arts of all kinds and who thought that they could encourage and inspire his people. By 30 BCE Vergil had published the four *Georgics,* poems that taught about the life of a farmer. Augustus and Maecenas asked Vergil to write an epic poem about Rome that would restore a sense of national pride and self-esteem in a people who had suffered one hundred years of civil war. Vergil spent the last ten years of his life in the Naples area working on the *Aeneid,* his epic poem about Aeneas, a Trojan hero who survived the fall of Troy and followed the command of the gods to cross the Mediterranean Sea to the west, finally arriving in Italy and establishing a race of people who were destined to found Rome. Although the poem deals with the lives and difficulties of the dispossessed Trojans who lived long before Vergil, the real theme is the greatness of Rome and the sacrifices and hardships endured in her creation. When Vergil was dying he asked that the *Aeneid,* which he felt was incomplete, should be burned after his death. The Emperor Augustus disregarded this wish and had the poem published. In its incomplete state it is considered one of the finest epics ever written.

SECTION I

SUMMARY OF VERGIL'S *AENEID*

The *Aeneid* is divided into twelve books. It details the destruction of Troy and the struggles of Aeneas and his band of Trojan refugees while they were seeking the "Western Land" promised them by the gods. This book uses passages from Books I, II, IV, and VI; thus the summary of these is more detailed here.

The *Aeneid* begins when the Trojans, burned out of their native city by the Greeks and uncertain where the gods want them to go, have been wandering around the Mediterranean Sea for several years, trying to set up a new home in various lands. When they finally learn that they should go to Italy, the goddess Juno hopes to see to it that Aeneas does not arrive there to found the Roman race. She persuades, or rather bribes, the wind-god Aeolus to raise a storm that almost sinks the Trojan fleet near the coast of Africa. Neptune stops the storm, and Aeneas, tossed ashore, sets out with his faithful friend, Achates, to search for his lost ships and to find out where they have landed. His mother, Venus, comes to him in disguise and tells him he is near Carthage, a new city ruled by the widow Dido. Venus complains to Jupiter about the promises he has made about Aeneas' future greatness and sends her mischievous son Cupid to make Dido fall in love with Aeneas at a banquet the queen gives for the foreigners.

At the banquet Dido asks Aeneas to tell the story of the fall of Troy. Aeneas begins near the end of the war, when the Greeks, despairing of open attack on the walls, build a huge wooden horse, conceal soldiers in it, and leave it on the beach, while all the ships are hidden behind the nearby island of Tenedos. When the Trojans take the horse into the city, the Greeks sneak out of the horse and open the gates for their fellow Greeks. Aeneas awakes and fights until his mother tells him to flee with his family from the doomed city. Aeneas' father, Anchises, does not want to go with his son, feeling that, since the gods have allowed his home to be destroyed, he has no hope, but signs from the gods change his mind. Aeneas' wife is lost in the confused escape, and the new widower evades the Greeks within the city and gathers the remnants of the Trojans around him to flee.

2 · VERGIL FOR BEGINNERS

Next Aeneas tells of the wanderings of the Trojans as they sail west from Troy. After several attempts to build a home fail, the household gods tell Aeneas that the land he seeks is Italy. After several other unfortunate landings they come to Sicily, where Anchises dies. Aeneas concludes by saying that when they set sail once more, a great storm drove them to Africa.

After the banquet Dido falls more and more deeply in love with Aeneas; she shares everything with him and stops overseeing the rising city. Her city's walls are not being built, the defenses are not being raised; everything is at a standstill. This is very dangerous, as Dido and her small band of Phoenicians are strangers in North Africa who have recently come to the land and are living in a small area reluctantly granted to them by the Africans. As though that were not enough, her brother, Pygmalion, who murdered her husband, King Sychaeus, in order to get his gold, is likely any day to pursue Dido and her band to Africa in search of that gold, which they carried away with them. Juno wants Aeneas to marry Dido and defend Carthage instead of founding Rome, so she approaches Venus with a plan for a royal marriage. Venus agrees, knowing that this plan will make Dido's city safe for Aeneas and that the Fates, assisted by nudges from Jupiter, will see to it that he ultimately sails for Italy. Once Dido and Aeneas have begun a romance, Jupiter dispatches Mercury to Africa to send Aeneas about his business, which is founding Rome. Mercury finds Aeneas, decked out in a jeweled sword and a fine cloak that Dido had given him, overseeing the building projects in Carthage. The messenger god blasts this "henpecked" behavior and reminds Aeneas in no uncertain terms that his duty is to his Trojans, his son, and to his destiny. Despite the agony he knows this will bring to Dido, and in spite of the love he feels for her, Aeneas obeys the gods. As he faces her accusations and pleas with unyielding purpose, she becomes more and more deranged. She places a comprehensive curse on Aeneas and all his descendants before she commits suicide.

Aeneas sails to Sicily and holds a royal funeral for his father Anchises. While this is in progress, Juno sends Iris to persuade the Trojan women to set fire to the ships rather than set sail once more, but Jupiter sends a rainstorm to save the fleet. Inspired by Minerva, the Trojans advise Aeneas to leave the weary ones in Sicily and set sail with the rest. Anchises appears to Aeneas in a dream and agrees with this advice, but also asks his son to come to the world of the dead and consult him. Aeneas sets out with the strongest Trojans for Italy.

When Aeneas arrives in Italy, he visits the Sybil of Apollo at Cumae to request the trip to the Underworld. After he has performed the necessary duties to the gods, the Sybil guides Aeneas into Hades. With the reluctant cooperation of the elderly boatman, Charon, they cross the Styx and see many people Aeneas recognizes, including the shade of Dido. Passing Tartarus, they arrive at the Elysian Fields and find Anchises. After an enthusiastic greeting, Anchises explains that some souls after being purified are chosen to drink from Lethe, the river of forgetfulness, and return to earth. Discussing the reincarnated souls who will become Romans gives him a chance to foretell the greatness of Rome, after which he sends Aeneas on his way with renewed purpose.

Back in Italy again, Aeneas and his Trojans sail northward to the River Tiber. Here they meet the aged king Latinus, his wife Amata, and their one child, the princess Lavinia. Queen Amata wants Lavinia to marry the Rutulian leader Turnus, but Latinus, troubled by omens that have indicated that Lavinia should marry a foreign hero, welcomes the Trojans and offers Lavinia to Aeneas in marriage. Juno, enraged at the possible success of Aeneas' work, sends the Fury Allecto to drive Amata and Turnus to desperate measures against the Trojans. War begins, and both Aeneas and Turnus find allies among the Italians.

After much bloodshed and much interference by the gods, King Latinus asks for a truce for the burial of the dead. Aeneas replies that his feelings for the Latins are friendly and that he would have preferred to meet Turnus in single combat. His justice and moderation are much admired by the Latins, and the truce is made.

Aeneas and Turnus finally meet in a one-on-one combat. While the two engage in single combat, Jupiter urges Juno to give up her hostility toward the Trojans. She agrees, with the stipulation that the Latins shall retain their name and language and that the Trojans shall be absorbed into their race. Turnus falls, and asks for mercy. Aeneas is moved to spare his life, but he sees that Turnus is wearing as a trophy the armor of Aeneas' gallant young friend Pallas, whom Turnus had killed without mercy. In anger and grief Aeneas kills Turnus.

SE<TION II

PLAYLET

THE MANY WORLDS OF AENEAS
A SET OF DUET ACTING SCENES FROM THE AENEID
(BOOKS I, II, IV, AND VI)

This little play both spoofs and summarizes major scenes of Books I, II, IV, and VI of the *Aeneid*. It may be performed or read before assigning the literature studies that follow, so that students might better understand the action. The performance will also point out that the ancients, though they felt that the gods had great power and brought good or bad things to them, at the same time scolded the gods from time to time and called them to account if prayers were not answered.

The scenes are short enough to learn easily for presentation if desired, and they involve a number of participants without putting undue strain on anyone. Extra non-speaking roles can be added to fit class enrollment so that everyone has some part. Various winds can be sitting around during the Juno-Aeolus scene, for example; there can be family members and servants in Anchises' palace; there may be spirits or even trees in Elysium, etc. Simple props and costume items to suggest the various characters are sufficient. Examples are a mirror for Venus, a crown for Juno, and a trident for Aeolus.

* * * * * * * * * * * *

(At the beginning and the end of scenes, a Narrator/Stage Manager character sets the scene and provides closure.)

DRAMATIS PERSONAE

Narrator/Stage Manager

Achates

Aeneas

Aeolus

Anchises

(Ascanius)

(Creusa)

Juno

Venus

SCENE I
THE WINDS OF OLYMPIAN WAR
(Selection 1: Book I)

Narrator/Stage Manager: Long ago, right after the Greeks made such a mess of the city of Troy, Prince Aeneas gathered the refugees he could find and sailed away from Asia Minor to seek a new home, as he had been directed by the gods to found a new city. As his instructions had been a bit skimpy in such details as location, he spent several years wandering the Mediterranean trying to discover where this new home was to be. When he did get on the right track, Juno, Queen of Heaven and Past Mistress of the Fine Art of Grudge-Holding, decided to torpedo the plans, and, if she could get around the decrees of the Fates, torpedo Aeneas as well.

(Aeolus is seated on a rock, carefully drawing a weather map. Juno enters and speaks.)

Juno: Hail, Aeolus!

(Aeolus turns slowly from his work, does a double take, jumps to his feet, and then falls to his knees.)

Aeolus: Mother Juno! Great Queen of Heaven! What in Hades . . . . I mean, how can I serve you, great Queen of the Gods?

Juno: I wish you to use your winds.

Aeolus: Certainly, ma'am. Right away, ma'am. Er—which winds?

Juno: All of them.

Aeolus: ALL!?! Do you realize what a calamity that would stir up?

Juno: A calamity is exactly what I want. Here. *(She points to the map.)* North/northeast of Carthage. What's left of Troy is in the Tyrrhene Sea, carrying their conquered gods to Italy. Sink them!

Aeolus: Sink them, my lady?

Juno: Sink them, waterlog them, overwhelm them, drown them, GET RID OF THEM!

Aeolus: But Aeneas . . . Jupiter . . . the prophecies of the Fates . . . .

Juno: Granted, it will be a difficult task with certain risks. I have noticed that you, ah, approve of Deiopea?

Aeolus: *(with a bright, eager look)* Deiopea?

Juno: Must you repeat everything I say? Are you a demi-god or a recording machine? Yes, Deiopea, the loveliest of my nymphs, idiot! Don't tell me you haven't been sighing over her. Do my will and she's yours.

Aeolus: Naturally I shall do your will, O Great Queen of the Gods.

Juno: *(with lifted eyebrow)* I rather thought you would.

Aeolus: Er . . . you will cover all this with Jupiter?

Juno: Do your part—I'll take care of the rest.

(Aeolus bows low as Juno sweeps out.)

SCENE II
AFOOT IN A STRANGE LAND
(Selection 2: Book I)

Narrator/Stage Manager: Aeolus did his part with enthusiasm. Raising his spear, he struck the mountainside, and all the winds roared forth together. The next thing the Trojans knew, everything went black, the waves were rising to the sky (or where the sky would probably be if one could still see it), and topsy and turvy were badly scrambled. Neptune, brought forth from the depths of his sea by the noise, brought the storm to a screeching halt. Aeneas' people, those in the seven ships that were still in evidence that is, drew up the boats at the nearest coast, rinsed the salt water and sand out of their teeth, and prepared such a supper as they could from their scanty and somewhat waterlogged provisions. Next morning Aeneas felt he needed to try to find the other thirteen ships and get a little information about the shore he had washed up on.

> *(At dawn, Aeneas is leaving camp. Achates scrambles after him, carrying his bow and arrows.)*

Achates: Aeneas! Where are you going?

Aeneas: Morning, Achates. How do you feel?

Achates: How do I feel? Like I've been pickled in salt water. Even if I can get rid of the salt crust, I doubt that I'll ever get really dry again. But you aren't getting me off the subject. At the risk of repeating myself, where are you going?

Aeneas: I hope I can find a high place and maybe spot some of the rest of our ships. Besides, I need to find out where we are and who or what lives here, before we find out the hard way.

Achates: *Noblesse oblige* again. Just because you are the ranking prince, you not only have to provide for everybody, but take all the risks as well. I'm glad I'm nobody special.

Aeneas: Well, if you're nobody special, go back and catch a little more sleep.

Achates: You know I tag along wherever you go to carry your weapons and try to keep you out of trouble. You're such a noble hothead.

Aeneas: I'm not ten years old, you know.

Achates: No, when you were ten you had more sense. Why not take a scouting party?

Aeneas: Because I'm a little afraid of what we may find.

Achates: Shipwrecks, for example?

Aeneas: That, or a war party. The two of us can move quietly and see what's out there.

Achates: The only moving thing I see is that trio of stags over there.

Aeneas: Giants! One of them would supply meat for a ship. And there's a whole flock behind them! Don't just stand there! Hand over that bow!

(Achates hands over the weaponry.)

Achates: Got one, got two—there goes number three. How many do you intend to shoot? They look a tad heavy for toting back to camp.

Aeneas: I'll shoot one for each ship. Run back and tell the men they're here, and I don't think we'll have to worry about transportation for the meat.

Achates: Bagged another one! OK. I'll go get the men. Harebrained you may be, but you're a first class shot.

SCENE III
THE DEPARTURE FROM TROY
(Selection 3: Book II)

Narrator: Aeneas, with considerable help from his mother, Venus, found the city of Carthage and greatly impressed Dido, its young and beautiful widowed queen. Queen Dido gave a banquet for Aeneas and his followers. As far as the future of Carthage was concerned, that proved to be a bad move, for Venus sent Cupid disguised as Ascanius to make Dido fall hopelessly in love with Aeneas. Already beginning to feel the effects of Cupid's work, Dido insisted that Aeneas tell all about his adventures. He began at the end of the war, with the construction of the Trojan horse and its lamentable aftermath, and explained that, jerked out of a sound sleep in his father's suburban villa, he fought his way across the city until called back by his mother to save his family. When he got back to the house, he found Anchises feeling peevish. When Aeneas started to pick up his father and carry him out of the city, Anchises announced that the rest of them could go, but he preferred to be reduced to a cinder along with Troy. "If the gods wanted me to live," he opined, "they shouldn't have burned my home." This was Too Much. Aeneas announced that he would die in battle and was only stopped by his wife Creusa, who had also had Too Much. She grabbed him around the knees and got terribly in the way of his getting back to battle. While he was untangling himself and trying to stay on his feet, she held up his little son and begged for a father's pity. This melodramatic scene was made still more melodramatic by the flame that suddenly began to play around the child's head, licking his temples but causing him no harm. His parents hurriedly put out this little conflagration with water, but it had a strange effect on the tyke's grandfather.

(Anchises is seated centerstage; Aeneas stands near him looking frustrated; Creusa and Ascanius are standing on Aeneas' other side.)

Anchises: This was a sign—a sign from the gods!

Aeneas: They set the boy's hair on fire? Wasn't that a little drastic?

Anchises: *(ignoring Aeneas, raising his hands palm outward, and looking toward the sky)* All-powerful Jupiter, if you listen to any prayers, look down on us, and if we earn your notice by our devotion, give us help, Father, and confirm this holy sign.

Aeneas: *(muttering to himself)* I hope the Omnipotent Father is in a mood to listen. So far tonight he hasn't been exactly helpful. (*Creusa pokes him, and he jumps as thunder sounds on the left.*)

Anchises: *(pointing out the window)* Look! A falling star! It's making the night as bright as day! There it goes, over the roof and behind Mount Ida!

Aeneas: And its track smells to high Heaven of sulphur.

Anchises: *(struggling to raise himself from his chair)* My praises to the holy star. I'll go wherever you want, gods of my fathers. Save my house, save my grandson! This sign is from you; now I know you have a future for Troy.

Aeneas: I don't think I'll ever understand the older generation.

Anchises: *(turning to Aeneas)* Why are you just standing there, Son, with your mouth open? Get a move on! I'm waiting to follow wherever you lead.

SCENE IV
THE AFTEREFFECTS OF LOVE
(Selection 4: Book IV)

Narrator: While Aeneas was finishing the story of his past seven years, Cupid/Ascanius completed his sneaky work, and Dido went down for the count. She lost all interest in the day-to-day business of building a city and a society, and behaved in a sickeningly romantic manner, which soon drew Juno's attention up on Mount Olympus. Correctly surmising that Venus was behind all this, the Queen of the Gods descended on Venus' Olympian palace.

> *(Venus is seated, checking her makeup. In her mirror she sees Juno enter behind her, gives a little start, and decides that the best defense is offense.)*

Venus: Juno, why are you always meddling in other people's affairs?

Juno: What do you mean, why am I always meddling? Speak for yourself, dearest Venus!

Venus: I'm only protecting my son. My motives are pure!

Juno: You wouldn't know a pure motive if it spilled all over you! *(momentarily diverted)* How DO you manage to look so radiant? What were you smearing on your face just now? Give it to me.

Venus: Don't change the subject! It wasn't enough that you did your best to drown my son; you had to shipwreck Aeneas in Africa and throw him at Dido. If that isn't meddling, what is?

Juno: Well, that was no excuse for your sending Cupid to shoot Dido with that nasty arrow and turn her to mush. Just look at her! She's pathetic! She spends every day showing your precious son the work that has been done in Carthage, and every night she gives another of those dreary banquets and has him tell his life story all over again.

Venus: Well, it's a very touching story. He has suffered enough hardships to make any woman love and pity him. And whose fault is that?

(Juno draws herself up to her full height and Venus hastily tries another tack.)

Venus: Why don't you just consider it a nice relaxation for her after all the hard work of building your city?

Juno: Relaxation? When she wanders through the palace after every banquet looking at the moon with a goofy expression, and then lies down on his dining couch and tries to picture him? It would take a Romantic poet, and a pretty maudlin one at that, to appreciate that scene!

Venus: She'll get over that once he sails for Italy.

Juno: No hurry about that, is there? Why can't he just stay in Carthage and marry Dido? They can rule the city together.

Venus: Over my dead—*(Juno glares at her)*. On second thought, dear Queen of the Gods, perhaps it might be a good idea. *(fuming, in an undervoice)* This is nothing but a plot to derail Aeneas from founding New Troy! *(with a little aside smirk)* Do you think you can get Father Jupiter's permission for this?

Juno: Leave that to me. I hope I know how to handle my own husband.

(Juno goes regally out.)

Venus: That's a forlorn hope. Especially if I get to him first.

SCENE V
THE FUTURE OF ROME
(Selections 5 and 6: Book VI)

Narrator: True to his promise, Anchises did follow where Aeneas led, for seven long years. He died in Sicily (probably of exhaustion) shortly before Aeneas set out on that ill-fated voyage that ended in Dido Country. A minor inconvenience like death did not keep him from exerting his influence on Aeneas' affairs, however. When Venus prodded Jupiter into cutting short Dido's romantic hopes and hurrying Aeneas off to Italy, Anchises added his bit by appearing in his son's dreams and ordering him to go fulfill his destiny. Later he also commanded Aeneas to come visit him in the Underworld for further instruction. When Aeneas landed in Italy, his first port of call was the cave of the Cumaean Sybil, a rather daunting priestess of Apollo who had a standing passport to the World of the Dead. This was a hard thing to come by, as Hades did not encourage the tourist trade, but, after Aeneas, with a bit of help from Venus, found the single golden bough in the forest that would serve as his entry visa, she guided him through this dismal world to the single bright spot, Elysium, where the good dead resided. Here he found Anchises.

(Anchises is standing looking off across Elysium, contemplating the future. Aeneas comes up beside him.)

Aeneas: Father?

Anchises: *(holding out both hands)* So you have come at last? It must have been a tough trip, but I hoped your loyalty (or curiosity) would hold out long enough to make it. So it's really possible to see you again? To talk to you again?

Aeneas: Obviously it is.

Anchises: I knew you could do it! I have been counting the days, and at last I have what I wished for.

Aeneas: You didn't look much like you had what you wished for when I walked up. Tell me, what were you studying so hard about?

Anchises: I was taking a survey of the souls destined to be born into the upper world again, and at the moment I was concentrating on my descendants and what they will be up to. I don't think much of some of them—they are tough, and strong, and definitely determined, but they need some goal definition.

Aeneas: What do you want them to do?

Anchises: Fulfill their unique destiny and not try to be like other people.

Aeneas: Not even good people?

Anchises: Especially good people! Some nations, I think, will make statues of bronze and marble so lifelike they seem to breathe, but that is not for Romans.

Aeneas: Romans?

Anchises: That is what our descendants will be called. Other nations will map the heavens and foretell the movements of the stars—but that is not for Romans.

Aeneas: So what are they supposed to do?

Anchises: Remember, Roman, your art is to rule the nations—to impose the habit of peace, to spare the humble, and to break the proud!

Aeneas: That is one tall order!

Anchises: Yes, but if they fill it, they will be unique among peoples, and they will shape the world for all time to come.

Aeneas: Then let's hope it works out—and that they have a first-rate poet to tell about it.

Narrator/Stage Manager: So Anchises went on surveying souls, and Aeneas set out to recreate Troy in Italy. He had his work cut out for him, but the Fates had decreed that Rome should rise, and, Juno notwithstanding, rise she did. Many thanks for your attention, friends. May your voyages never be stormy, and all your loves end happily, and may your descendants fulfill all your hopes.

S€<TION III

Reading Latin Poetry

The beginning of this book noted that Vergil in telling his story of the founding of Rome wrote the *Aeneid* as a very long poem of the kind called epic. Poetry and music appear to have arisen from a common ancestor, perhaps the chant. Poetry in any language tends to follow rhythm patterns of that language, putting them in a stylized form. Poetry may or may not rhyme in English; in Classical Latin, rhymes generally are not used.

Rhythm and Meter

The natural rhythm of English (that is the pattern into which the most words fall when spoken naturally) is iambic (one unstressed syllable followed by one stressed one)—probably pentameter (five sets of unstressed/stressed to a line). Read these lines from Robert Frost's *Birches:*

> When I see birches bend to left and right
>
> Across the line of straighter, darker trees,
>
> I like to think some boy's been swinging them.

Read aloud these lines of Edna St. Vincent Millay's sonnet on WWII, in which she longs to leave her world as Aeneas left Troy:

> I straighten back in weariness, and long
>
> To gather up my little gods and go.

One of the most powerful and widely used English poetry forms is blank verse, which is iambic pentameter (five feet per line, each foot having one unstressed syllable followed by a stressed one) without rhyme. *Birches* is written in blank verse.

The natural rhythm of Latin in the hands of poets such as Vergil seems to have adapted well to dactylic (one stressed, or in Latin one long, syllable followed by two unstressed, or in Latin short, ones)—probably hexameter (six sets of long, short, short syllables in a line), or at least longer lines than we find in English. Practicing reading in this meter helps students pronounce long Latin words. Although in Latin poetry we are speaking of true long and short syllables, while in English we are not concerned with how long they are but whether they are stressed or unstressed, the principle can still help us in both languages. Although they do not occur very often, there are English poems written in dactyls, some in shorter verses, some in hexameters.

The following lines from Longfellow's *Hiawatha's Childhood* are trochaic tetrameter (four sets of long/short syllables to a line):

> Downward through the evening twilight,
>
> In the days that are forgotten,
>
> In the unremembered ages,
>
> From the full moon fell Nokomis,
>
> Fell the beautiful Nokomis,
>
> She a wife, but not a mother.

Read these lines aloud, saying the words normally and stressing the ones stressed in ordinary speech.

The lines of English poetry below from Longefellow's *Evangeline* are written in dactylic hexameter:

> Then came the laborers home from the field, and serenely the
>   sun sank.
>
> Softly the Angelus sounded, and over the roofs of the village
>
> Columns of pale blue smoke, like clouds of incense ascending,
>
> Rose from a hundred hearths, the homes of peace and
>   contentment.

Read each of the Longfellow passages above aloud in English.

Now, in reading the Latin lines below, we find that certain words are elided (run together, with the last syllable of the first word dropping out). This happens when one word ends with a vowel or vowel +*m* and the next word begins with a vowel.

> Example: *magna insula:*   *magn(a)insula*
>
>   *magnam insulam:*   *magn(am)insulam*

The skipped or elided vowel is neither pronounced nor counted. We also need to know which vowels are naturally long and which are long by position (because they are followed by two consonants—not necessarily in the same word).

The long vowels in the lines below are marked. Above each syllable is a symbol denoting long or short.

    _ ∪∪ _ _   _ _   _ _   _ ∪∪ _ _
    incute / vim ven / tīs sub / mersās / qu(e) obrue / puppēs,

    _ ∪∪ _ _ _ _ _∪∪ _ ∪∪ _ _
    aut age dīver sōs et dīsice corpora pontō.

Read the lines aloud.

Below are the Latin lines for the Selection 1 reading passage with the long vowels marked. The length of the syllables is marked in the first two lines. Practice reading two lines aloud at a time.

    _∪∪/ _   ∪ ∪/_ _/_ ∪∪ /_   ∪ ∪/_ _
    "Aeole, namque tibī dīvum pater atqu(e h)ominum rēx

    _ _/ _∪ ∪/_ _ /_ _/_ _/_ ∪∪/_ _
    et mulcēre dedit flūctūs et tollere ventō,

    gēns inimīca mihī Tyrrhēnum nāvigat aequor,

    Īlium in Ītaliam portāns victōsque Penātēs:

    incute vim ventīs submersāsque obrue puppēs,

    aut age dīversōs et dīsice corpora pontō.

    sunt mihi bis septem praestantī corpore nymphae,

    quārum quae fōrmā pulcherrima Dēiopēa,

    cōnūbiō iungam stabilī propriamque dicābō."

SECTION IV

Passages for Comprehension

Suggested study approaches:

1. Begin by reviewing Scene I of *The Many Worlds of Aeneas.*

2. Consult the Reading Latin Poetry section, and read through the Selection 1 Latin passage (which is also featured in the Reading Latin Poetry Section) just for the sound.

3. Go through the Latin-to-Latin Vocabulary and Vocabulary Aids.

   OR

   Do the Carpe Grammaticam section for Selection 1, using the word bank; then go through the Latin-to-Latin Vocabulary and Vocabulary Aids.

4. Discuss what the passage says in general.

   OR

   Translate the passage.

5. Do the comprehension and discussion questions individually or as a group.

(Special Note: Since this is poetry, which was a relative of music and meant to be read aloud, we must take extra care in matching word endings to understand the meaning of clauses and phrases, as the poet scatters words about as one would not do in a line of prose. He uses unusual arrangements of words to produce sound effects and word pictures; in addition, he is writing in a definite metrical pattern, so that he must have a certain arrangement of long and short syllables.)

SELECTION 1: BOOK I, LINES 65–73
Juno's Promise to Aeolus

In the seventh year after the Trojan War, the Trojans had finally learned that their target destination was Italy. They happily set out for that land, but Juno was determined to stop them. The Fates had decreed that Aeneas would be the ancestor of the Romans, and the Fates always had their way. But Juno thought there must be an exception to every rule. Off she went to the Mountain of the Winds on the island Aeolia to have a chat with King Aeolus, who ruled the winds. Jupiter had imprisoned all the winds there for fear that they might do great damage to the world and to humankind. Juno indicated that she wanted Aeolus to interfere with the Trojan plans, made a few pointed suggestions, and promised him a special reward if he did what she asked.

Fig. 1. Juno visits Aeolus.

Latin-to-Latin Vocabulary

Try to use these Latin synonyms for words in the passage before using the English vocabulary aids. These Latin synonyms are of course not exact equivalents but will help you to understand the passage.

Line 65

> **tibī** dat. of **tū**
> **dīvum** deōrum

Line 66

> **mulcēre** facere quiētum
> **flūctūs** undae
> **tollere** excitāre

Line 67

> **gēns** populus
> **inimīca** nōn amīca
> **mihī** dat. of **ego**
> **aequor** mare

Line 68

> **Īlium** Trōiam
> **Penātēs** deōs

Line 69

> **incute** iace (mitte)
> **vim** violentia
> **obrue** oppugnā
> **puppēs** navēs

Line 70

> **dīsice** iace
> **pontō** marī

Line 71

> **mihi** dat. of **ego**
> **bis septem** quattuordecim
> **praestantī** pulchrō

Line 72

> **quārum** gen.f.pl. of **quī**
> **quae** f. of **quī**

Line 73

> **cōnūbiō** mātrimōniō
> **dicābō** dābō

Aeneid, Book I, lines 65–73

Juno greets Aeolus, king of the winds, and tells him about the Trojans and what she would like him to do.

"Aeole, namque tibī dīvum pater atque hominum rēx	65
et mulcēre dedit flūctūs et tollere ventō,	
gēns inimīca mihī Tyrrhēnum nāvigat aequor,	
Īlium in Ītaliam portāns victōsque Penātēs:	
incute vim ventīs submersāsque obrue puppēs,	
aut age dīversōs et dīsice corpora pontō.	70

Juno promises Aeolus a bribe if he succeeds.

sunt mihi bis septem praestantī corpore nymphae,
quārum quae fōrmā pulcherrima Dēiopēa,
cōnūbiō iungam stabilī propriamque dicābō, . . ."

Vocabulary Aids

namque for
dīvum of gods
hominum of men
tibī to you
atque and
mulcēre to soothe
dedit has granted, has given
flūctūs waves of the sea
tollere to stir them up
inimīca unfriendly, hostile
mihī to me
Īlium city of Troy
portāns carrying
victōsque Penātēs the conquered household gods

vim force
ventīs to the winds
submersās puppēs the waterlogged ships
dīsice throw
pontō into the sea
sunt mihi (dat. of possession) I have
bis septem twice seven (fourteen)
praestantī excellent
quārum of whom
quae the one
pulcherrima most beautiful
propriam (with **eam** understood) your very own

COMPREHENSION QUESTIONS

1. What title does Juno use for her husband Jupiter?

2. What powers has Jupiter given to Aeolus?

3. What does Juno say that the Trojan race is bringing to Italy?

4. What does she want Aeolus to do?

5. What will be his reward?

DISCUSSION AND EXPLORATION QUESTIONS

1. We have mentioned that Vergil uses word placement to form pictures; therefore, sometimes adjectives are not next to the nouns they modify. In line 67, what word does *Tyrrhēnum* go with? How does *Tyrrhēnum nāvigat aequor* give a picture of what is happening in the line?

2. In line 68, what does *Īlium* mean? In what sense does Aeneas *portat Īlium*?

3. What are the Penates? Why does Juno say they are *victōs*?

Selection 2: Book I, lines 184–193
Aeneas' Provision for His Men
after They Escape the Storm

Aeneas with seven of his ships limped into harbor in North Africa near Carthage after Neptune put an end to Aeolus' attempt to drown the Trojans and win himself a bride. At dawn, after a hasty meal of grain saved from the sea and a good night's rest, Aeneas began to wonder where they had landed. Concealing his ships in the harbor, he set out to find out where they were. Aeneas took one friend (who would forever be known as the faithful Achates) and set out, looking for his other ships and exploring the land. The first thing he found provided more food for his people.

Fig. 2. Aeneas and Achates take in the scenery.

LATIN-TO-LATIN VOCABULARY

Use these synonyms to help you understand the passage before you go to the Vocabulary Aids.

Line 184
> conspectū vīsū
> nūllam nōn
> lītore ōrā

Line 185
> prōspicit spectat
> errantēs currentēs
> hōs m.pl. of hic, haec, hoc
> armenta gregēs
> sequuntur (post) veniunt

Line 186
> ā tergō post hōs
> agmen grex
> pāscitur cibum capere

Line 187
> cōnstitit stetit
> hīc in locō

Line 188
> corripuit cēpit
> quae n.pl. of quī
> gerēbat portāvit

Line 189
> ductōrēs ducēs
> ipsōs m.pl. of ipse
> ferentēs portantēs

Line 190
> sternit necat
> vulgus gregem

Line 191
> miscet excitat
> nemora silvam
> turbam multitūdinem

Line 192
> abstitit cessit
> ingentia magna

Line 193
> fundat necet
> humī in terrā
> aequet aequōs fēcit

AENEID, BOOK I, LINES 184–193

Aeneas scans the sea and then the land.

nāvem in cōnspectū nūllam, trēs lītore cervōs
prōspicit errantēs; hōs tōta armenta sequuntur   185
ā tergō, et longum per vallēs pāscitur agmen.

He decides to provide food for his people.

cōnstitit hīc, arcumque manū celerēsque sagittās
corripuit, fīdus quae tēla gerēbat Achātēs;
ductōrēsque ipsōs prīmum, capita alta ferentēs
cornibus arboreīs, sternit, tum vulgus, et omnem   190
miscet agēns tēlīs nemora inter frondea turbam;
nec prius abstitit quam septem ingentia victor
corpora fundat humī et numerum cum nāvibus aequet.

VOCABULARY AIDS

cōnspectū sight	**ductōrēs** leaders
nūllam no	**ipsōs** themselves
lītore on the shore	**ferentēs** bearing, wearing
errantēs running	**arboreīs** like trees
hōs these	**sternit** (he) kills
sequuntur (they) follow	**vulgus** crowd, herd
ā tergō from the back	**agēns** driving
agmen line	**turbam** the crowd
pāscitur (it) is eating	**nemora** woods
cōnstitit he stopped	**abstitit** (he) stopped
hīc here	**nec prius . . . quam** not until
manū in his hand	**ingentia** huge
corripuit (he) snatched up	**fundat** he stretches out
quae (things) which	**humī** on the ground
gerēbat (he) was carrying	**aequet** he equals

COMPREHENSION QUESTIONS

1. When Aeneas went looking for his ships, what did he find instead?

2. What did he immediately take from his friend Achates?

3. Who were his first victims?

4. What was the reaction of the rest?

5. How many did Aeneas kill?

DISCUSSION AND EXPLORATION QUESTIONS

1. Why does Vergil say that the *ductōrēs* had *cornua arborea?* What does this indicate about them?

2. Why does Aeneas kill seven *cervōs?*

SELECTION 3: BOOK II, LINES 687–704
Signs from the Gods and Departure from Troy

At Dido's banquet Aeneas explains that he woke up to find the city in flames and fought his way across it until called back by his mother to save his family. At home, when Aeneas started to pick up his father and carry him out of the city, Anchises refused to go. "If the gods wanted me to live," he said, "they shouldn't have burned my home." Aeneas announced that he would go back to die in battle and was only stopped by his wife Creusa, who, holding their little son Iulus/Ascanius, begged for a father's pity. A flame suddenly began to play around the child's head, licking his temples but causing him no harm. Anchises recognized a sign from the gods, and asked for another sign to confirm the first.

Fig. 3. Anchises asks a sign from the gods.

LATIN-TO-LATIN VOCABULARY

Use these synonyms to help you understand the passage before you go to the Vocabulary Aids.

Line 687
at sed
sīdera stellās
laetus beātus

Line 688
extulit (with oculōs) spectāvit
palmās manibus
tetendit intendit

Line 689
precibus verbīs sacrīs
flecteris movēris

Line 690
aspice spectā
nōs acc.pl. of ego
hoc n. of hic
pietāte factīs bonīs

Line 691
haec n.pl. of hic
ōmina signa
firmā cōnfirmā

Line 692
ea n.pl. of is
senior comp. of senex
fātus erat dīxerat
fragōre sonitū

Line 693
intonuit surrēxit
laevum sinistrum
lāpsa from lābor

Line 694
facem ignem
cucurrit from currō

Line 695
illam f.acc. of ille
summa altissima (super. of altus)
lābentem from lābor
culmina verticēs
tēctī domūs

Line 696
cernimus vidēmus
sē acc. of suī
condere pōnere

Line 697
sīgnantem dēmōnstrantem
sulcus vestīgium
līmite fīne

AENEID, BOOK II, LINES 687–698
Father Anchises asks for guidance.

at pater Anchīsēs oculōs ad sīdera laetus
extulit et caelō palmās cum vōce tetendit:
'Iuppiter omnipotēns, precibus sī flecteris ūllīs,
aspice nōs, hoc tantum, et sī pietāte merēmur,   690
dā deinde auxilium, pater, atque haec ōmina firmā.'

The sign from the gods comes.

vix ea fātus erat senior, subitōque fragōre
intonuit laevum, et dē caelō lāpsa per umbrās
stella facem dūcēns multā cum lūce cucurrit.
illam summa super lābentem culmina tēctī   695
cernimus Īdaeā clāram sē condere silvā
sīgnantemque viās; tum longō līmite sulcus
dat lūcem et lātē circum loca sulphure fūmant.

VOCABULARY AIDS

at but	**laevum** on the left side
sīdera stars	**lāpsa** falling
laetus happy	**dūcēns** leading
caelō to the sky	**facem** flame, torch
palmās (his) hands	**summa** the highest
precibus by prayers	**lābentem** gliding
ūllīs any	**culmina** highest points
flecteris you are moved, affected	**tēctī** of the house
aspice look	**cernimus** we see
ōmina omens, signs from the gods	**sē** itself
firmā confirm	**condere** to hide
ea these things	**sīgnantem** pointing out
senior older man, old man	**līmite** course, path
fātus erat he had spoken	**sulcus** the way, the journey
fragōre with a crash	**lūcem** light
intonuit it thundered	**fūmant** (they) smoke, fume

LATIN-TO-LATIN VOCABULARY

Use these synonyms to help you understand the passage before you go to
the Vocabulary Aids.

Line 699
   genitor pater
   tollit (with **sē ad aurās**) stat

Line 700
   adfātur vocat
   sīdus stella

Line 701
   sequor veniō post
   quā ubi

Line 702
   dī patriī deī patriae
   nepōtem fīlium fīlī

Line 703
   hoc n. of **hic**
   vestrum dē vōbīs
   augurium signum
   nūmine potestāte

Line 704
   cēdō moveor
   nāte fīlī
   tibī dat. of **tū**
   comes socius
   īre prōcēdere
   recūsō negō

AENEID, BOOK II, LINES 699–704
Anchises changes his mind.

> hīc vērō victus genitor sē tollit ad aurās
> adfāturque deōs et sanctum sīdus adōrat.   700
> 'iam iam nūlla mora est; sequor et quā dūcitis adsum,
> dī patriī; servāte domum, servāte nepōtem.
> vestrum hoc augurium, vestrōque in nūmine Trōia est.
> cēdō equidem nec, nāte, tibī comes īre recūsō.'

VOCABULARY AIDS

genitor father

tollit sē ad aurās got up and stood

adfātur he addresses

sīdus star

quā where

dī patriī gods of the fatherland

vestrum, vestrō your (pl.)

augurium sign, omen

nūmine in the power, in the will

cēdō I yield

nāte son

comes companion

īre to go

recūsō I refuse

COMPREHENSION QUESTIONS

1. What position did Anchises take for prayer?

2. What does he ask from the gods?

3. What sound and what sight were signs from the gods?

4. What other sense besides sight and hearing witnessed the sign?

5. What was Anchises' reaction?

6. What did he say to the gods?

7. What did he say to Aeneas?

DISCUSSION AND EXPLORATION QUESTIONS

1. How does Anchises' position for prayer contrast with that usually shown in modern times?

2. What condition does he attach to asking for his gods' help?

3. Research the significance of *intonuit laevum.*

SELECTION 4: BOOK IV, LINES 74–83
Dido's Love for Aeneas

After the banquet that Queen Dido had given for Aeneas (and to which Mother Venus had sent her son Cupid disguised as Iulus to infect the poor queen with love for Aeneas), Dido spent a wretched night, longing for Aeneas and recalling the oath of eternal fidelity she had sworn at the time of her husband Sychaeus' death. She rose from her night couch in misery. Suddenly everything in her world revolved around the foreigner, and she began to behave more like a lovesick schoolgirl than a ruling queen.

Fig. 4. Dido shows Aeneas the city of Carthage.

Latin-to-Latin Vocabulary

Use these synonyms to help you understand the passage before you go to the Vocabulary Aids.

Line 74
> **sēcum** cum sē
> **moenia** murōs

Line 75
> **Sīdoniāsque** Pūnicās
> **ostentat** dēmōnstrat
> **opēs** pecūniam

Line 76
> **effārī** dīcere
> **resistit** subsistit

Line 77
> **eadem** from **idem**
> **lābente** from **lābor**
> **quaerit** petit

Line 78
> **Īliacōs** Trōiānōs
> **iterum** rūrsus
> **dēmēns** sine mente

Line 79
> **exposcit** postulat
> **pendet** amat
> **nārrantis** dīcentis
> **ōre** verbīs

Line 80
> **dīgressī (sunt)** exiērunt
> **lūmenque** lūx
> **obscūra** pallida

Line 81
> **premit** condit
> **suādent** persuādent

Line 82
> **maeret** dolet
> **stratīsque** lectō

Line 83
> **incubat** reclīnat (with **in**)
> **illum** from **ille**
> **absēns, absentem** pres. part. of **absum**

AENEID, BOOK IV, LINES 74–83
Dido and Aeneas tour Carthage.

nunc media Aenēān sēcum per moenia dūcit
Sīdoniāsque ostentat opēs urbemque parātam,   75
incipit effārī mediāque in vōce resistit;

Dido is lost in love.

nunc eadem lābente diē convīvia quaerit,
Īliacōsque iterum dēmēns audīre labōrēs
exposcit pendetque iterum nārrantis ab ōre.
post ubi dīgressī, lūmenque obscūra vicissim   80
lūna premit suādentque cadentia sīdera somnōs,
sōla domō maeret vacuā strātīsque relīctīs
incubat. illum absēns absentem auditque videtque, . . .

VOCABULARY AIDS

Aenēān acc. of Aeneas	**pendet** hangs upon
moenia fortifications	**nārrantis** of (the one) telling
sēcum with her	**ōre** the words
Sīdoniās Carthaginian	**dīgressī (sunt)** they have gone out
ostentat (she) shows, exhibits	**lūmen** light
opēs wealth, resources	**obscūra** fading
effārī to speak	**vicissim** in turn
resistit (she) stops	**suādent** they advise
convīvia banquet, party	**somnōs** (poetic plural) sleep
quaerit she requests	**maeret** she grieves
iterum again	**strātīs** dining couch
dēmēns heedless	**incubat** she lies upon
exposcit (she) demands	**illum** Aeneas

Comprehension Questions

1. What is Dido showing to Aeneas?

2. How does she show her confusion of mind?

3. As each day ends, what does she do?

4. Why does she do this?

5. What does she do after the banquet is over?

Discussion and Exploration Questions

1. Dido is not crazy. Why does Vergil say she is *dēmēns?*

2. Read line 81 aloud. How do the sounds suggest the meaning of the line?

3. Line 83 uses two well-known figures of speech: a derivative form of anaphora, which is the repetition of a word, and polysyndeton, which is using more conjunctions than are really needed. How do they help show Dido's state of mind?

SELECTION 5: BOOK VI, LINES 679–691
Aeneas' Visit to Anchises in Elysium

Prompted by visits from the god Mercury, Aeneas left Carthage with more haste than dignity. Having escaped the perils of wedlock in Africa, he land-ed in Italy and made the hazardous trip to the Underworld to get a bit of advice from his father Anchises, who was now residing in Elysium. After an eventful journey through Hades in which he confronted mournful Trojans, defiant Greeks, and a contemptuous Dido, Aeneas finally arrived at Ely-sium. Here he was relieved to see that, unlike the gloomy grey atmosphere of the rest of Hades, sunlight and green plants abounded. The blessed souls of heroes and public benefactors were dancing, singing, wrestling, working out with weights, and doing all the things they had enjoyed in life. One Musaeus, the biggest of the crew, obligingly pointed him in the general di-rection in which Anchises most probably would be found. In the lush green valley to which he had been directed, Aeneas interrupted Anchises, who was surveying souls due to return to earth.

Fig. 5. Aeneas greets Anchises as they meet in Elysium.

LATIN-TO-LATIN VOCABULARY

Use these synonyms to help you understand the passage before you go to the Vocabulary Aids.

Line 679
   at sed
   penitus in
   convalle valle intrā montēs
   virentī viridī

Line 680
   inclūsās praetectās
   animās spīritūs
   lūmen lūx
   itūrās from eō

Line 681
   lūstrābat spectābat
   recolēns putāns (with **dē**)

Line 682
   recēnsēbat numerābat
   cārōs amātōs
   nepōtēs fīliōs

Line 683
   virum virōrum
   mōrēs from mōs
   manūs facta

Line 684
   is from is, ea, id
   tendentem venientem
   adversum ad eum
   grāmina herbās

Line 685
   alacris m.s., celer
   tetendit extendit

Line 686
   effūsae fūsae
   genīs ōrae
   excidit vēnit (with **ex**)

Line 688
   vīcit from vincō
   tuērī vidēre

Line 689
   nāte fīlī
   reddere permūtāre

Line 690
   dūcēbam putābam (with **animō**)
   animō mente
   rēbar aestimābam

Line 691
   dīnumerāns numerāns
   mē from ego
   cūra dēsīderium
   fefellit from fallō

AENEID, BOOK VI, LINES 679–691
Father Anchises contemplates the future.

At pater Anchīsēs penitus convalle virentī
inclūsās animās superumque ad lūmen itūrās   680
lūstrābat studiō recolēns, omnemque suōrum
forte recēnsēbat numerum, cārōsque nepōtes
fātaque fortūnāsque virum mōrēsque manūsque.

Anchises is overjoyed to see Aeneas coming toward him.

isque ubi tendentem adversum per grāmina vīdit
Aenēān, alacris palmās utrāsque tetendit,   685
effūsaeque genīs lacrimae et vōx excidit ōre:
"vēnistī tandem, tuaque exspectāta parentī
vīcit iter dūrum pietās? datur ōra tuērī,
nāte, tua et nōtās audīre et reddere vōcēs?
sīc equidem dūcēbam animō rēbarque futūrum   690
tempora dīnumerāns, nec mē mea cūra fefellit."

VOCABULARY AIDS

at but	**excidit** (it) came forth
penitus deep within	**ōre** from his mouth
convalle enclosed valley	**tuērī** to see
virentī green, flourishing	**nāte** son
inclūsās enclosed, protected	**reddere** to exchange
animās souls	**dūcēbam** I was planning
adversum facing	**animō** in my mind
alacris m.s., eager	**futūrum** (what is) going to be
effūsae poured out, pouring	**dīnumerāns** counting
genīs down (his) cheeks	**cūra** hope

COMPREHENSION QUESTIONS

1. What special group is Anchises contemplating when Aeneas arrives?

2. What will they evidently become?

3. How does Anchises react when he sees Aeneas coming?

4. What does he ask him?

5. How does he show that he can scarcely believe that this has happened?

6. What has he been counting up even while he reviewed the *animās itūrās ad lūmen superum?*

DISCUSSION AND EXPLORATION QUESTIONS

1. Vergil here gives a belief in reincarnation. Does everyone go back to earth? (Review *Aeneid* summary, Book VI.)

2. Vergil once more employs polysyndeton (too many conjunctions). What effect does it create here?

3. Vergil never tells us that Anchises loved Aeneas. How does he show us?

SELECTION 6: BOOK VI, LINES 847–853
Destiny of Rome

Anchises pointed out the future Romans he was looking over when Anchises arrived in Elysium and gave a brief biography of some of the most important. He showed more than a little misgiving about some of their prospective activities, and presented them with some sage advice about developing their outstanding national qualities.

Fig. 6. Aeneas and Anchises view the future.

LATIN-TO-LATIN VOCABULARY

Use these synonyms to help you understand the passage before you go to the Vocabulary Aids.

Line 847
  excūdent fōrmābunt
  spīrantia similis vīvō hominī
  mollius comp. adv. of mollis
  aera metallum

Line 848
  vultūs ōra

Line 849
  meātūs mōtiōnēs

Line 850
  dīcent praedīcent

Line 851
  imperiō potestāte
  mementō from meminī

Line 852
  hae from hic, haec, hoc
  tibi dat. (of possession) from tū
  pācis from pāx
  mōrem from mōs

Line 853
  subiectīs victīs

AENEID, BOOK VI, LINES 847–853

Anchises explains the relationship between Rome and other nations.

"excūdent aliī spīrantia mollius aera
(crēdō equidem), vīvōs dūcent dē marmore vultūs,
ōrābunt causās melius, caelīque meātūs
dēscrībent radiō et surgentia sīdera dīcent: 850
tū regere imperiō populōs, Rōmāne, mementō
(hae tibi erunt artēs), pācisque impōnere mōrem,
parcere subiectīs et dēbellāre superbōs."

VOCABULARY AIDS

aliī others
vultūs faces
meātūs the motion, movement
radiō with a measuring rod
mementō remember (imperative)
hae these

tibi your
pācis of peace
mōrem custom, habit
subiectīs (dat. with parcere) the conquered
dēbellāre to subdue

COMPREHENSION QUESTIONS

1. In what two artistic achievements will others excel the Romans?

2. In what other three fields will others excel?

3. What must the Romans remember?

4. What three achievements will be the Romans' arts?

DISCUSSION AND EXPLORATION QUESTIONS

1. What does the use of the words *spīrantia* and *vīvōs* indicate about the skill of the *aliī?*

2. What kinds of skills are discussed in line 850?

3. The use of comparative adverbs qualifies or subdues the statements in the first four lines. What do they indicate about Roman skills?

4. How does line 853 indicate that the Romans are to achieve peace?

SE<TION V

CARPE GRAMMATICAM EXERCISES
(GRASP THE GRAMMAR)

SELECTION 1: BOOK I, LINES 65–73

[Grammar Stressed: Present and Future Active Tenses of the 1st and 3rd Conjugations (first and third person singular); Present Active Imperatives of the 1st and 2nd Conjugations; 1st, 2nd, 3rd Declensions]

Answer these questions, making use of the word bank at the end of this section.

I. PRESENT AND FUTURE ACTIVE TENSES OF 1ST AND 3RD CONJUGATIONS

The last few letters on a Latin verb tell us a great deal about the use of that verb in a sentence. *Nāvigat and iungit* are third person present tense singular verbs. What does the final -*t* on each one mean?

1. Translate *nāvigat* and *iungit*.

2. *Dicābō* and *iungam* are both first person singular future tense verbs. The difference in their endings reflects the conjugation of verbs to which they belong, which is indicated by the vowel before the -*re* on their second part in the word bank below. Translate each of them.

3. Match each of the following words to its English meaning, looking carefully at the words and explanations above.

   ____ a. *nāvigābō*   1. I dedicate

   ____ b. *iungō*   2. I shall sail

   ____ c. *dicō*   3. I shall drive

   ____ d. *agam*   4. I join

II. Present Active Imperatives of 1ˢᵗ and 3ʳᵈ Conjugations

1. Imperatives give a command. Their understood subject is "you," but they are translated using only the verb without any preposition. Translate these third conjugation present active imperatives into English:

    a. *incute*

    b. *obrue*

    c. *age*

2. Present active imperatives of first conjugation verbs are made by dropping the *-re* from the second principal part of the verb. Make and translate the imperative for each of these verbs:

    a. *nāvigō, nāvigāre*

    b. *dicō, dicāre*

III. 1ˢᵗ, 2ᴺᴰ, and 3ʳᵈ Declension Nouns and Adjectives

1. First declension nominative singular feminine nouns end in *-a*, as do nominative and accusative neuter plurals of all declensions. Using the word bank at the end of this section to determine their gender, divide this list of words into nominative singulars and accusative plurals:

    inimīca, corpora, fōrma, pulcherrima.

    nominative singular (3):

    accusative plural (1):

2. Each of these words is nominative singular. Translate each word and then change it into the nominative plural:

    a. *pater*

    b. *rēx*

    c. *fōrma*

    d. *gēns*

3. These words are in different cases. Match each word with its English translation:

____ a. *ventō*	1. the sea (nom.)
____ b. *puppēs*	2. bodies (acc.)
____ c. *aequor*	3. in the sea
____ d. *pontō*	4. by, with the wind
____ e. *nymphae*	5. in marriage
____ f. *cōnūbiō*	6. the decks, the ships (nom.)
____ g. *corpora*	7. nymphs (nom.)

4. In Latin literature, students who are still in early study often find the accusative singular ending looks very much like endings of another case, the genitive plural. Genitive words are possessive; they can be put into English in a phrase beginning with "of." Words ending in *-ōrum* or *-ārum* are genitive plural.

Divide the following list of words into four accusative singulars and two genitive plurals:

quārum, Īlium, hominem, dīv(ōr)um, Ītaliam, propriam

Accusative Singular   Genitive Plural

WORD BANK

Words here and in the glossary in the back of this book are given in standard Latin dictionary form. Nouns have nominative singular followed by genitive singular and gender. Verbs have four principal parts, although the third and fourth parts are not stressed in the first sections.

Nota Bene: For this selection only, all principal parts are given in full. For the other selections, common forms will be abbreviated.

aequor, aequoris, n., sea

agō, agere, ēgī, āctum, to drive

cōnūbium, conūbiī (ī), n., marriage

corpus, corporis, n., body

dicō, dicāre, dicāvī, dicātum, to make, dedicate

dīvus, dīvī, m., god

fōrma, fōrmae, f., form

gēns, gentis, f., race

homō, hominis, m., human being

Īlium, Īliī (ī), n., Troy

incutiō, incutere, incussī, incussum, to send forth, strike into

inimīcus, -a, -um, unfriendly (to)

iungō, iungere, iūnxī, iūnctum, to join

nāvigō, nāvigāre, nāvigāvī, navigātum, to sail

obruō, obruere, obruī, obrutum, to overwhelm

pater, patris, m., father

pontus, pontī, m., sea

pulcher, -ra, -rum, beautiful

puppis, puppis, f., the stern of a ship, a ship

rēx, rēgis, m., king

ventus, ventī, m., wind

SELECTION 2: BOOK I, LINES 184–193

[Grammar Stressed: Present and Imperfect Tenses of the 2nd and 3rd Conjugations (first and third person); Pronouns *hic* and *qui* (relative)]

Answer these questions, making use of the word bank at the end of the section.

I. PRESENT AND IMPERFECT TENSES OF 2ND AND 3RD CONJUGATIONS

1. *Prōspicit, miscet,* and *fundat* are all third person singular verbs. How can you tell?

2. Present tense third person singular verbs generally are formed by dropping *-re* from the second principal part and adding *-t*. *Fundat* is a special case; it looks like *nāvigat* because the vowel has been changed to show that it is subjunctive expressing an implied purpose.

   a. To which conjugations do *errat* and *miscet*, which are in simple indicative present, belong? How can you tell?

   b. Translate *errat* and *miscet.*

   c. If the *-t* on the end of the verbs is changed to *-nt*, they become plural. Translate *errant* and *miscent.*

3. *Gerēbat* is in the imperfect tense because this is a continued action that Achates was doing over a period of time. Such action is indicated in English by the helping verbs "was" or "were." In Latin the letters *ba* are added just before the personal ending.

   Write out in Latin:

   a. he was confusing (them)

   b. he was driving

   c. they were seeing at a distance

II. *Hic* and Its Pronouns; *Quī* with Nouns

(Note: Pronouns are declined in all three genders so that they can agree with all Latin nouns.)

1. *Hic* is the first form of a set of demonstrative pronouns—pronouns that point things out. It is often translated into English as "this," if singular, and as "these," if plural. Its ending agrees in number, case, and gender with the ending of the noun it refers to.

   Translate these phrases:

   a. *hōs cervōs*

   b. *hic homō*

   c. *haec capita*

   d. *in cōnspectū hōc*

2. *Quae* in this selection, like *quārum* in Selection 1, is a relative pronoun. This means that it relates or ties together two separate clauses or parts of the sentence. *Quae* can match either a singular feminine or a neuter plural noun. If it relates to a noun that is a person, it is translated "who" or "whom." If it relates to a noun that is not a person, it is translated "which."

   Translate these phrases:

   a. *puella quae venit*

   b. *armenta quae veniunt*

   c. *manus in quā habeō*

WORD BANK

agō, agere, ēgī, āctum, to drive, live, or spend

armentum, -ī, n., herd

caput, capitis, n., head

cervus, -ī, m., deer

cōnspectus, -ūs, m., sight, view

est (from **sum**)

errō, -āre, -āvi, -ātum, to wander

fundō, fundere, fūdī, fūsum, to lay out, lay low

gerō, gerere, gessī, gestum, to carry

habeō, habēre, habuī, habitum, to hold

hic, haec, hoc, this (man, woman, thing)

homō, hominis, m., human being, man

manus, -ūs, f., hand

misceō, miscēre, miscuī, mixtum, to mix, mix up; to confuse

prōspiciō, prōspicere, prōspexī, prōspectum, to see in the distance

puella, -ae, f., girl

quī, quae, quod, who, which, that

veniō, venīre, vēnī, ventum, to come

Selection 3: Book II, lines 687–704

[Grammar Stressed: Perfect Tense (active, passive, and deponent, third person); Pronouns *ego/nōs, tū/vōs*]

Answer these questions, making use of the word bank at the end of the section.

I. Perfect Tense Verbs

1. In the vocabulary lists given in this book, all verbs have four parts given. These are known as the four principal parts. The last two parts are used to make perfect tense (past tense) verbs. Since active perfect tense verbs are made from the third principal part, and passive perfect tense verbs are made from the fourth principal part, of the individual verb, conjugation structure does not really apply to them.

   Translate the following perfect tense singular verbs, consulting the word bank if you need to for the verb they come from and its meaning:

   a. *extulit*

   b. *tetendit*

   c. *ēlātus est*

   d. *crēta est*

   e. *fātus est* (deponent; i.e., translate as active)

2. While the perfect tense singular active adds only the letter *t* to the third principal part, the plural changes the final *i* to an *ē* and adds -*runt*. The perfect tense passive uses the present tense of *sum*.

   Translate:

   a. *extulērunt*

   b. *ēlatī sunt*

   c. *fātī sunt*

3. Make the following verbs in Latin:

   a. he looked at

   b. he was saved

   c. they led

II. PERSONAL PRONOUNS

The personal pronouns *ego* (plural, *nōs*) and *tu* (plural, *vōs*) refer to the person speaking and the person spoken to, respectively.

Translate the following:

   a. *tibī* (dative)

   b. *vōbīs* (two ways, dative and ablative)

   c. *mihī* (dative)

WORD BANK

aspiciō, aspicere, aspexī, aspectum, to look at

cernō, cernere, crēvī, crētum, to see, understand

dūcō, dūcere, dūxī, ductum, to lead

efferō, efferre, extulī, ēlātum, to lift up; to carry out

ego, meī, I; (pl.) **nōs,** we

for, fārī, fātus sum (deponent), to speak

servō, -āre, -āvī, -ātum, to save, conserve

tendō, tendere, tetendī, tentum, to extend

tū, tuī, you (s.); (pl.) **vōs,** you

SELECTION 4: BOOK IV, LINES 74–83

[Grammar Stressed: Present and Perfect Participles of the 1ˢᵗ and 3ʳᵈ Conjugations; Ablative Absolute; Pronouns *suī* and *īdem*]

Answer these questions, making use of the word bank at the end of the section.

I. PRESENT AND PERFECT PARTICIPLES

Participles are verb forms used as adjectives; therefore they are hybrids; that is, they have basic forms like verbs but the endings of adjectives. They have tense like verbs, but they have gender, case and number like nouns and adjectives. Present participles are made from present tense verb stems (the second principal part of the verb minus -*re*) plus the endings -*ns*, -*ntis*; they are declined in the third declension regular and generally translated into English with the ending "-ing." Perfect passive participles (there are no perfect active participles) are the fourth principal part of regular verbs with the first and second declension regular endings -*us* -*a* -*um*. They are generally translated by the last principle part of the corresponding English verb, with or without "having been."

1. Translate these participles:

    a. *lābēns*

    b. *cadentia*

    c. *relictīs*

    d. telling

2. Translate these phrases:

    a. *Aenēās absēns*

    e. (having been) prepared (f.nom.)

    b. *urbem parātam*

II. ABLATIVE ABSOLUTES

Latin often uses a noun and a participle, both in the ablative case, as an elliptical (abbreviated) extra sentence. This is called an ablative absolute. Example: *urbe relictā*, the city having been left behind.

Translate these ablative absolutes:

a. *diē lābente*

b. *homine relictō*

c. *strātīs parātīs*

III. PRONOUNS *SUĪ* AND *ĪDEM*

Īdem, like *hic* and *ille*, has forms to match gender and number of nouns.

Since *suī* is reflexive (it restates and emphasizes a previously used noun or pronoun), it has case endings, but no separate endings for gender or number.

Translate:

a. *eadem sīdera*

b. *eōsdem labōrēs*

c. *Lūna sē premit.*

d. *Hominēs sē vident.*

WORD BANK

absum, abesse, āfuī, āfutūrum, to be away; to be absent

cadō, cadere, cecidī, cāsum, to fall, sink

diēs, diēī, m., day

homō, hominis, m., human being, man

īdem, eadem, idem, the same

lābor, lābī, lāpsus sum (deponent), to slip away

labor, labōris, m., hardship

nārrō, -āre, -āvī, -ātum, to tell

parō, -āre, -āvī, -ātum, to prepare

premō, premere, pressī, pressum, to suppress; to hide

relinquō, relinquere, relīquī, relictum, to leave behind, abandon

sīdus, sīderis, n., star, constellation, heavenly body

strātum, -ī, n., couch, quilt, bed

suī, sibi, sē (reflexive pron.) himself, herself, itself or themselves

urbs, urbis, f., city

videō, vidēre, vīdī, vīsum, to see

SELECTION 5: BOOK VI, LINES 679–691

[Grammar Stressed: Imperfect Tense (all persons, active, passive, and deponent of the 1ˢᵗ, 2ⁿᵈ, 3ʳᵈ, and 4ᵗʰ conjugations); Present, Perfect, and Future Participles; Demonstrative Pronoun *is*]

Answer these questions, making use of the word bank at the end of the section.

I. IMPERFECT TENSE

Selection 2 illustrated how imperfect tense can be used for continued or interrupted action in the past while the perfect (complete) tense shows completed action. Since the imperfect tense is made from the present stem and has *ba* before its personal ending, it is sometimes easier to recognize than the perfect tense, which is made from the third principal part.

Translate:

a. *lūstrābat*

b. *recēnsēbant*

c. *veniēbās*

d. *vēnistī*

e. *rēbar*

f. *fallēbar*

g. *fefellit*

II. PRESENT, PERFECT, AND FUTURE PARTICIPLES

(Hint: review the explanation in the previous selection.)

As we have seen, present participles are made by adding *-ns, -ntis* to the base of a verb, and perfect participles are the fourth principal part of a verb. Future participles, which will have the endings of conjugations I and II, as do the perfect participles, are made by changing the *-us -a -um* ending of the perfect participle to *-ūrus -ūra -ūrum*. These can be translated "going to be" or "about to be." Verbs such as *sum,* which cannot be passive, sometimes have the future participle instead of a perfect participle as the fourth principal part.

Translate these singular participles into English and change each to plural:

a. *tendentem*

b. *exspectāta*

c. *itūrus*

III. DEMONSTRATIVE PRONOUN *IS*

The demonstrative pronoun *is,* like *hic* and *ille,* has forms to agree with genders, cases, and numbers of nouns. Its nominative singular forms are *is, ea, id,* and its accusative singular forms are *eum, eam, id.*

Translate the following:

a. *Eum audiō.*

b. *Eam audiō.*

c. *Is mē audit.*

WORD BANK

audiō, audīre, audīvī, audītum, to hear

eō, īre, iī or **īvī, itum,** to go, sail, pass

exspectō, -āre, -āvī, -ātum, to await, expect

fallō, fallere, fefellī, falsum, to deceive

is, ea, id, he, she, it, this, that

lūstrō, -are, -āvī, -ātum, to check, examine; to purify

recēnseō, recēnsēre, recēnsuī, recēnsum, to count, enumerate

reor, rērī, ratus sum, to think, regard; to consider

sum, esse, fuī, futūrum, to be

tendō, tendere, tetendī, tentum, to move toward; to extend or stretch out

veniō, venīre, vēnī, ventum, to come

SELECTION 6: BOOK VI, LINES 847–853

[Grammar Stressed: Future Tense (third person of the 1st and 3rd conjugations and *sum*); Comparative Adverbs]

Answer these questions, making use of the word bank at the end of the section.

I. FUTURE TENSE

1. First and second conjugation verbs make their future tenses by adding *b* plus a vowel to the present stem (second part minus -*re*) before the personal ending. Third and fourth conjugation verbs make the future tense by changing the vowel before the personal ending to an *e* in every form except the first personal singular, which Selection 1 demonstrated.

   Translate these plural verbs into English; then change them to singulars and translate the result:

   (Hint: In the first conjugation verb, the *u* becomes an *i*.)

   a. *excūdent*

   b. *dūcent*

   c. *ōrābunt*

   d. *dēscrībent*

2. *Sum* is an irregular verb. Its future is made, not from its simple second principal part, but by using the stem *er-*. "You (s.) will be" is *eris*.

   Translate these forms:

   a. *erit*

   b. *erunt*

II. COMPARATIVE ADVERBS

Adjectives and adverbs in Latin, as in English, explain the thoughts of the language user more precisely. Adjectives refine the meaning of nouns and pronouns, while adverbs refine the meaning of verbs and adjectives. "He is coming slowly" *(venit tardē)* gives us more information than simply "he is coming" *(venit)*. Such statements can gain even more precision if compared to something or someone: "he is coming more slowly than I did" *(venit tardius quam ego vēnī)*. In Latin as in English adverbs are often made from adjectives; thus comparative adverbs take the ending *-ius* attached to the base of the parent adjective.

Translate these phrases:

a. *regent melius*

b. *dīcent mollius*

WORD BANK

dēscrībō, dēscrībere, dēscrīpsī, dēscrīptum, to describe, sketch out

dīcō, dīcere, dīxī, dictum, to say, speak, tell, recite

dūcō, dūcere, dūxī, ductum, to bring forth

excūdō, excūdere, excūdī, excūsum, to hammer out

melius, adj. and adv., comp. of **bonus,** better

mollis, mollis, molle, gentle, graceful

ōrō, -āre, -āvī, -ātum, (with **causās**) to plead cases

regō, regere, rēxī, rēctum, to rule, guide

sum, esse, fuī, futūrum, to be

ABBREVIATIONS

abl.	ablative
acc.	accusative
adj.	adjective
adv.	adverb
comp.	comparative
conj.	conjunction
dat.	dative
def.	defective
f.	feminine
gen.	genitive
indecl.	indeclinable
intens.	intensive
m.	masculine
n.	neuter
num.	numerical
pl.	plural
pres. part.	present participle
pron.	pronoun
semidep.	semideponent
s.	singular
super.	superlative

GLOSSARY

A

ā, ab, prep.+ abl., *by, with, from, (named) after*

absistō, absistere, abstitī, –, *to withdraw, cease*

absum, abesse, āfuī, āfutūrum, *to be away; to be absent*

Achātēs, -ae, m., *Aeneas' companion*

ad, prep.+ acc., *to, toward, near*

adfor or affor, adfārī, adfātus sum, *to address, speak to*

adōrō, -āre, -āvi, -ātum, *to worship, adore*

adsum, adesse, adfuī, adfutūrum, *to be near, be present*

adulescēns, adulescentis, m., *young man, young person*

adversum, prep.+ acc., *facing, towards*

Aenēās, -ae, m., *Trojan hero, son of Venus and Anchises*

Aeolus, -ī, m., *Aeolus, king of the winds*

aequō, -āre, -āvi, -ātum, *to make equal; to equate; to regard as an equal*

aequor, aequoris, n., *sea, smooth sea*

aequus, -a, -um, *even; steady; calm*

aes, aeris, n., *bronze, copper*

ager, agrī, m., *field*

agmen, agminis, n., *line of movement or march, army column*

agō, agere, ēgī, āctum, *to do, drive, live, or spend*

alacer or alacris, alacris, alacre, *quick, eager*

alius, -a, -ud, *another;* pl., *others*

altus, -a, -um, *high, deep*

amor, amōris, m., *love*

Anchīsēs, -ae, m., *father of Aeneas*

anima, -ae, f., *soul, life*

animus, -ī, m., *mind, will*

aqua, -ae, f., *water*

arbor, arboris, f., *tree*

arboreus, -a, -um, *treelike, branching*

arcus, arcūs, m., *bow, curve, arch*

arma, -ōrum, n.pl., *weapons, arms*

armentum, -ī, n., *herd*

ars, artis, f., *skill, work of art*

arx, arcis, f., *citadel, fortress*

ascēndō, ascēndere, ascēndī, ascēnsum, *to climb*

aspiciō, aspicere, aspexī, aspectum, *to look at*

at, conj., *but*

atque, conj., *and*

audiō, audīre, audīvī, audītum, *to hear, listen; to be within hearing*

augurium, -iī (ī), n., *augury, observation of signs and omens*

aura, -ae, f., *the air, the heights*

aut, conj., *or;* aut . . . aut, *either . . . or*

auxilium, -iī (ī), n., *help, aid*

B

beātus, -a, -um, *happy, blessed*

bellum, -ī, n., *war*

bis, num. adv., *twice*

C

cadō, cadere, cecidī, cāsum, *to fall, be slain*

caelum, -ī, n., *sky, heavens*

canō, canere, cecinī, cantum, *to sing*

capiō, capere, cēpī, captum, *to take, grasp, occupy; to exact*

caput, capitis, n., *head; capital (of a country)*

cārus -a, -um, *dear*

causa, -ae, f., *cause, reason, case*

cēdō, cēdere, cessī, cessus, *to go, go away; to cease; to yield*

celer, celeris, celere, *swift*

cernō, cernere, crēvī, crētum, *to see, understand*

cervus, -ī, m., *deer*

cibus, -ī, m., *food*

circum, prep.+ acc., *around*; adv., *about, all around*

clāmō, -āre, -āvi, -ātum, *to shout, proclaim*

clārus, -a, -um, *famous; bright, clear*

collum, -ī, n., *neck*

comes, comitis, m./f., *companion, friend*

commisceō, commiscēre, commiscuī, commixtum, *to mix together; to confuse*

condō, condere, condidī, conditum, *to establish*

cōnfirmō, cōnfirmāre, cōnfirmāvī, cōnfirmātum, *to strenghthen, confirm*

coniugium, -iī (ī), n., *union, marriage*

cōnscius, -a, -um, *aware of, privy to*; m./f., *partner, confederate*

cōnspectus, cōnspectūs, m., *sight, view*

cōnstō, -āre, constitī, –, *to stand firm, stop*

contingō, contingere, contigī, contāctum, *to touch*

cōnūbium, -iī (ī), n., *marriage*

convallis, convallis, f., *enclosed valley*

convīvium, -iī (ī), n., *banquet*

cornū, cornūs, n., *horn*

corpus, corporis, n., *body*

corripiō, corripere, corripuī, correptum, *to snatch up, seize*

crēdō, crēdere, crēdidī, crēditum, + dat., *to believe, entrust to*

culmen, culminis, n., *summit, height*

culpa, -ae, f., *fault, blame*

cum, prep.+ abl., *with, among*; conj., *when, since, although*

cūra, -ae, f., *care, concern, desire*

currō, currere, cucurrī, cursum, *to run*

D

Dardanidēs, -ae, m., *descendant of Dardanus; Trojan*

Dardanius, -a, -um, *Trojan*

dē, prep.+ abl., *down from; out of*

dēbellō, -āre, -āvī, -ātum, *to subdue, wear down*

deinde, adv., *from there, then*

Dēiopēa, -ae, f., *one of Juno's nymphs*

dēmēns, dēmentis, *out of one's mind; reckless*

dēmōnstrō, -āre, -āvī, -ātum, *to show*

dēscrībō, dēscrībere, dēscrīpsī, dēscrīptum, *to describe, sketch out*

deus, -ī, m., *god*

dicō, -āre, -āvī, -ātum, *to give, dedicate*

dīcō, dīcere, dīxī, dictum, *to say, speak, tell, recite*

Dīdō, Dīdōnis, f., *foundress and queen of Carthage*

diēs, diēī, m., *day*

dīgredior, dīgredī, dīgressus sum, *to separate; to move away*

dīnumerō, -āre, -āvī, -ātum, *to count up*

dīsiciō, dīsicere, dīsiēcī, dīsiectum, *to scatter, throw*

dīversus, -a, -um, *separate, in different directions*

dīvidō, dīvidere, dīvīsī, dīvīsum, *to divide, distribute*

dīvus, -ī, m., *god*

dō, -are, dedī, dātum, *to give; to make*

domus, domūs, f., *home, house*

dūcō, dūcere, dūxī, ductum, *to lead; to bring forth; to plan*

ductōr, ductōris, m., *leader*

dūrus, -a, -um, *hard, harsh, difficult*

dux, ducis, m., *leader*

E

efferō, efferre, extulī, ēlātum, *to lift up; to carry out*

effor, effārī, effātus sum, *to speak, speak out*

effundō, effundere, effūdī, effūsum, *to pour out*

ego, meī, *I*

enim, conj., *for (generally not first word)*

eō, īre, iī or īvī, itum, *to go; (of time) to pass; to ride, sail*

equidem, adv., *truly, of course*

errō, -āre, -āvī, -ātum, *to wander*

et, conj., *and; et . . . et, both . . . and*

excidō, excidere, excidī, –, *to come out, fall out*

excitō, -āre, -āvī, -ātum, *to stir up, excite*

excūdō, excūdere, excūdī, excūsum, *to hammer out*

exeō, exīre, exiī or īvī, exitum, *to go out*

exposcō, exposcere, expoposcī, –, *to demand, insist upon*

exspectō, -āre, -āvi, -ātum, *to await, expect*

extendō, extendere, extendī, extensum, *to stretch out, extend*

F

faciō, facere, fēcī, factum, *to do, make*

factum, -ī, n., *deed*

fallō, fallere, fefellī, falsum, *to deceive*

fāma, -ae, f., *reputation, fame*

fātālis, fātāle, *destined, fated, deadly*

fātum, -ī, n., *destiny, fate*

fax, facis, f., *torch*

ferō, ferre, tulī, lātum, *to bear, carry*

fidus, -a, -um, *faithful*

fīlius, -iī (ī), m., *son*

fīnis, fīnis, m., *boundary, border*

firmō, -āre, -āvī, -ātum, *to strengthen, reinforce*

flectō, flectere, flēxī, flectum, *to turn, bend*

flūctus, flūctūs, m., *wave*

for, fārī, fātus sum, *to speak*

fōrma, -ae, f., *figure, beauty*

fŏrmō, -āre, -āvī, -ātum, *to shape*

forte, adv., *by chance (from* fors, fortis, f.)

fortūna, -ae, f., *fortune, luck*

fragor, fragōris, m., *crash, noise, uproar*

frangō, frangere, frēgī, frāctum, *to break*

frondeus, -a, -um, *leafy*

fūmō, -āre, -āvī, -ātum, *to smoke*

fundō, fundere, fūdī, fūsum, *to pour, lay out, lay low*

furor, furōris, m., *blind rage, fury*

G

gaudeō, gaudēre, gāvīsus sum, semidep., *to rejoice*

gena, -ae, f., *cheek*

genitor, genitōris, m., *father*

gēns, gentis, f., *family, tribe, nation*

gerō, gerere, gessī, gestum, *to bear; to entertain (feelings); to wear, carry on*

grāmen, grāminis, n., *grass*

grandō, grandinis, f., *hail*

grex, gregis, m., *flock, herd*

H

habeō, habēre, habuī, habitum, *to hold*

hīc, adv., *here*

hic, haec, hoc, *this (man, woman, thing)*

homō, hominis, m., *human being, man;* m.pl., *people*

humilis, humile, *low, humble, poor*

humus, -ī, f., *earth*

I

iaciō, iacere, iēcī, iactum, *to throw, hurl*

iam, adv., *now, already*

Īdaeus, -a, -um, *Idaean, pertaining to Mt. Ida near Troy*

īdem, eadem, idem, *the same*

ignis, ignis, m., *fire*

Īliacus, -a, -um, *Trojan*

Īlium, -iī (ī), n., *Troy*

ille, illa, illud, *that (man, woman, thing)*

impendeō, impendēre, –, *to threaten; to be near at hand*

imperium, -iī (ī), n., *authority, mastery*

impetus, impetūs, m., *attack*

impōnō, impōnere, imposuī, impositum, *to impose; to set in place*

in, prep.+ abl., *in, on; among;* + acc., *into, onto; towards*

incautus, -a, -um, *reckless, heedless*

incipiō, incipere, incēpī, inceptum, *to begin*

inclūdō, inclūdere, inclūsī, inclūsum, *to shut in, include*

inclutus, -a, -um, *famous*

incubō, -āre, incubuī, incubitum, + dat., *to lie upon*

incutiō, incutere, incussī, incussum, *to strike*

infēlīx, (infēlīcis), *unfortunate, unhappy*

ingēns, (ingentis), *great, huge*

inimīcus, -a, -um, *unfriendly (to)*

insequor, insequī, insecūtus sum, *to follow*

instō, -āre, institī, –, *to follow through, carry out*

intendō, intendere, intendī, intentum (sum), *to stretch out, fasten*

inter, prep.+ acc., *between, among*

intereā, adv., *meanwhile*

intonō, -āre, intonuī, intonitum, *to thunder forth*

intrā, prep.+ acc., *inside, within*

intrō, -āre, -āvī, -ātum, *to enter*

ipse, ipsa, ipsum, intens. pron., *himself, herself, itself;* intens. adj., *very, precisely*

is, ea, id, *he, she, it, this, that*

Ītalia, -ae, f., *Italy*

iter, itineris, n., *journey, march; route*

iterum, adv., *again*

iungō, iungere, iūnxī, iūnctum, *to join;* **sē iungere** (+ dat.) *to join (someone or something)*

Iūno, Iūnōnis, f., *Juno, wife of Jupiter and queen of the gods*

Iuppiter, Iovis, m., *chief god of the Romans*

iuventūs, iuventūtis, f., *youth; (collectively) young people*

L

lābor, lābī, lāpsus sum, *to slip, glide, slip away*

labor, labōris, m., *effort, work, hardship*

lacrima, -ae, f., *a tear (from the eye)*

laetus, -a, -um, *happy*

laevum, -a, -um, *left (side), on the left*

lātus, -a, -um, *wide*

lectus, -ī, m., *couch, bed*

līmen, līminis, n., *threshold, doorway, entrance*

līmes, līmitis, m., *trail, track*

lītus, lītoris, n., *seashore*

locus, -ī, m. (pl. n.), *place*

longus, -a, -um, *long*

lūceō, lūcēre, lūxī, –, *to shine*

lūmen, lūminis, n., *light*

lūna, -ae, f., *moon*

lūstrō, -āre, -āvī, -ātum, *to check, examine; to purify*

lūx, lūcis, f., *light*

M

māchina, -ae, f., *large mechanism, machine*

maereō, maerēre, –, *to grieve*

magnus, -a, -um, *great, large*

malus, -a, -um, *evil*

manus, manūs, f., *hand; handiwork; deeds*

mare, maris, n., *sea*

marmor, marmoris, n., *marble*

mātrimōnium, -iī (ī), n., *marriage*

meātus, meātūs, m., *motion*

meditor, meditārī, meditātus sum, *to think over, reflect upon*

medius, -a, -um, *middle (of)*

melius, adj. and adv., comp. of **bonus**, *better*

meminī, meminisse, def. (*imperative* **mementō**), *to remember*

mēns, mentis, m., *mind*

mereō, merēre, meruī, meritum, *to deserve, earn;* abl.+ **de**, *to serve, render service to*

metallum, -ī, n., *metal*

metus, metūs, m., *fear*

meus, -a, -um, *my, mine*

minor, minārī, minātus sum, *to threaten*

misceō, miscēre, miscuī, mixtum, *to mix, mix up; to disturb; to confuse*

moenia, moenium, n.pl., *fortifications, town walls*

mollis, molle, *gentle, graceful*

mōns, montis, m., *mountain*

monstrum -ī, n., *wonder, monstrosity*

mora, -ae, f., *delay*

mors, mortis, f., *death*

mōs, mōris, m., *habit, custom;* pl., *character*

mōtiō, mōtiōnis, f., *motion*

moveō, movēre, mōvī, mōtum, *to move*

mulceō, mulcēre, mulsī, mulsum, *to soothe; to appease*

multitūdō, multitūdinis, f., *great number*

multus, -a, -um, *many*

murmur, murmuris, n., *a murmur, a rumbling*

mūrus -ī, m., *wall*

N

namque, conj., *for truly*

nārrō, -āre, -āvī, -ātum, *to tell*

nātus, - ī, m., *son*

nāvigō, -āre, -āvī, -ātum, *to sail*

nāvis, nāvis, f., *ship*

nec, (adv. not conj.) *and not, nor;* nec … nec, *neither … nor;* nec iam, *no longer*

necō, -āre, -āvī, -ātum, *to kill*

negō, -āre, -āvī, -ātum, *to deny, refuse*

nemus, nemoris, n., *grove of trees*

nepōs, nepōtis, m., *grandson; descendant*

nōmen, nōminis, n., *name*

nōn, adv., *not*

nōs, *we, us*

nōtus, -a, -um, *well-known, familiar*

nūllus, -a, -um, *no; nonexistent;* pron., *none*

nūmen, nūminis, n., *will, consent, divine power*

numerus, -ī, m., *number*

nunc, adv., *now*

nympha, -ae, f., *nymph (demi-goddess)*

O

obruō, obruere, obruī, obrutum, *to overwhelm, strike*

obscūrus, -a, -um, *dark, fading*

oculus, -ī, m., *eye*

ōmen, ōminis, n., *omen, sign, prophecy*

omnipotēns, (omnipotentis), *all-powerful*

omnis, omne, *every, all*

opēs, opium, f.pl., *wealth, resources*

oppugnō, -āre, -āvī, -ātum, *to attack, strike*

opus, operis, n., *work*

ōra, -ae, f., *seacoast*

ōrō, -āre, -āvī, -ātum, *to beg, plead*

ōs, ōris, n., *mouth, voice, words*

ostentō, -āre, -āvi, -ātum, *to show, exhibit*

P

pallidus, -a, -um, *pale, wan*

palma, -ae, f., *palm of the hand, hand*

pandō, pandere, pandī, pānsum, *to spread open, open*

parcō, parcere, pepercī, parsūrum, *to spare, show mercy to*

parēns, parentis, m., *parent, ancestor*

parō, -āre, -āvī, -ātum, *to prepare, provide*

pars, partis, f., *part*

pāscor, pāscī, pāstus sum, *to graze, eat*

passim, adv., *here and there*

pater, patris, m., *father*

patria, -ae, f., *native land*

patrius, -a, -um, *of the native land*

pāx, pācis, f., *peace*

pecūnia, -ae, f., *money, property, possessions*

Penātēs, Penātium, m.pl., *Penates, household gods*

pendeō, pendēre, pependī, –, *to hang upon; to hesitate*

penitus, adv., *deep within*

per, prep.+ acc., *through, along, during*

persuādeō, persuādēre, persuāsī, persuāsum, *to suggest; to persuade*

pēs, pedis, m., *foot*

petō, petere, petīvī, petītum, *to seek, ask for, apply for*

pietās, pietātis, f., *devotion to gods, family and country*

plēnus, -a, -um, *full (of)*

pōnō, pōnere, posuī, positum, *to put, place*

pontus, -ī, m., *the sea*

populus, -ī, m., *a people, a nation*

porta, -ae, f., *city-gate; entrance*

portō, -āre, -āvī, -ātum, *to carry*

post, prep.+ acc., *behind, after*

postulō, -āre, -āvi, -ātum, *to demand*

potestās, potestātis, f., *power*

praedīcō, praedīcere, praedīxī, praedictum, *to tell beforehand; to predict*

praestō, -āre, praestitī, praestitum, *to be outstanding or excellent*

premō, premere, pressī, pressum, *to press, suppress; to hide*

prex, precis, f., *prayer*

prīmum, adv., *at first, in the first place, for the first time*

prīmus, -a, -um, *first*

priusquam, conj., *before*

prōcēdō, prōcēdere, prōcessī, prōcessum, *to go forward, proceed*

prōnuba, -ae, f., *matron of honor at a wedding*

proprius, -a, -um, *one's own, particular*

prōspiciō, prōspicere, prōspexī, prōspectum, *to see in the distance, spot*

puella, -ae, f., *girl*

puer, puerī, m., *boy*

pulcher, -ra, -rum, *beautiful*

Pūnicus, -a, -um, *Punic, Phoenician, Carthaginian;* Pūnicī, -ōrum, m.pl., *Carthaginians*

puppis, puppis, f., *stern, ship*

putō, -āre, -āvī, -ātum, *to think*

Q

quā, adv., *where? how?*

quaerō, quarere, quaesīvī, quaesītum, *to look for, seek*

quattuordecim, indecl., *fourteen*

-que, enclitic ending, *and*

quī, quae, quod, *who, which, that*

quiētus -a -um, *quiet*

R

radius, -iī (ī), m., *ray, spoke, measuring rod*

recēnseō, recēnsēre, recēnsuī, recēnsum, *to count, enumerate*

reclīnō, -āre, -āvī, -ātum, *to lean back, rest*

recolō, recolere, recoluī, recultum, *to think over, consider*

recūsō, -āre, -āvī, -ātum, *to refuse*

reddō, reddere, redidī, redditum, *to give back, exchange*

regō, regere, rēxī, rēctum, *to rule, guide*

relinquō, relinquere, relīquī, relictum, *to leave behind, abandon*

reor, rērī, ratus sum, *to think, regard; to consider*

resistō, resistere, restitī, –, *to stop, stand still; to pause*

rēx, rēgis, m., *king*

Rōmānus, -a, -um *Roman; (noun) a Roman*

ruō, ruere, ruī, rutum, *to rush, sweep headlong*

rūrsus, adv., *again*

S

sacer, -ra, -rum, *holy, sacred*

sacrātus, -a, -um, *hallowed, consecrated*

sagitta, -ae, f., *arrow*

sānctus, -a, -um, *consecrated, holy*

scandō, scandere, scandī, –, *to climb, ascend*

sēcrētus, -a, -um, *concealed, secret*

sed, conj., *but*

senex, senis, *aged;* m., *old man*

septem, indecl., *seven*

sequor, sequī, secūtus sum, *to follow*

servō, -āre, -āvī, -ātum, *to save, conserve*

sī, conj., *if*

sīc, adv., *so, as*

Sīdonius, -a, -um, *Sidonian, Phoenician*

sīdus, sīderis, n., *star, constellation, heavenly body*

sīgnō, -āre, -āvī, -ātum, *to signify, express*

signum, -ī, n., *sign, standard*

silva, -ae, f., *forest*

sine, prep.+ abl., *without*

sinister, -ra, -rum, *left hand, on the left side*

sistō, sistere, stetī or **stitī, statum,** *to cause to stand, place, establish*

socius, -iī (ī), m., *ally, companion*

sōlus, -a, -um, *only, single, alone*

somnus, -ī, m., *sleep*

sonitus, sonitūs, m., *sound, noise*

sonus, -ī, m., *sound*

speciēs, speciēī, f., *appearance, position*

spectō, -āre, -āvī, -ātum, *see, catch sight of*

spēlunca, -ae, f., *cave*

spīrō, -āre, -āvī, -ātum, *to breathe*

stabilis, stabile, *steadfast, enduring*

stella, -ae, f., *star*

sternō, sternere, strāvī, strātum, *to spread out, overthrow*

stō, -āre, stetī, statum, *to stand*

stomachus, -ī, m., *stomach, entrails*

strātum, -ī, n., *couch, quilt, bed*

studium, -iī (ī), n., *eagerness*

suādeō, suādēre, suāsī, suāsum, *to suggest, propose*

sub, prep.+ abl., *under, beneath;* + acc., *beneath*

subeō, subīre, subīvī or subiī, subitum, *to enter*

subiciō, subicere, subiēcī, subiectum, *to throw under, subject, conquer*

subitō, adv., *suddenly*

submergō, submergere, submersī, submersum, *to sink, submerge*

subsistō, subsistere, substitī, –, *to stop, take a stand*

suī, sibi, sē, *himself, herself, itself* or *themselves*

sulcus, -ī, m., *track, trail, furrow*

sulphur or sulfur, sulphuris, n., *sulphur*

sum, esse, fuī, futūrum, *to be*

summus, -a, -um, *the highest*

super, prep.+ acc., *over, above*

superbus, -a, -um, *the arrogant, the haughty*

superus, -a, -um, *upper*

surgō, surgere, surrēxī, surrēctum, *to rise*

sustineō, sustinēre, sustinuī, –, *to hold up; to endure*

suus, sua, suum, *his, her, its* or *their own*

T

tamen, adv., *nevertheless, yet*

tandem, adv., *at last, finally*

tangō, tangere, tetigī, tāctum, *to touch*

tantum, adv., *so much, only*

tēctum, -ī, n., *roof; shelter; house*

tegō, tegere, tēxī, tēctum, *to cover, protect*

tēlum, -ī, n., *weapon*

tempus, temporis, n., *time*

tendō, tendere, tetendī, tentum, *to extend; to move toward*

tergum, -ī, n., *the rear*

timor, timōris, m., *fear, dread*

tollō, tollere, sustulī, sublātum, *to lift, raise; to destroy*

tonitrus, tonitrūs, m., *thunder*

tōtus, -a, -um, *whole, entire*

transverberō, -āre, –, *to pierce through, transfix*

trēs, tria, *three*

Trōia, -ae, f., *Troy*

Trōiānus, -a, -um, *Trojan*

tū, tuī, *you (s.)*

tueor, tuērī, tuitus (tūtus) sum, *to look at, regard; to guard*

tum, adv., *then*

turba, -ae, f., *great throng, mob; disturbance, uproar*

tuus, -a, -um, *your*

Tyrrhēnum, -ī, n., *Tyrrhene Sea (between Western Italy and the islands of Sicily and Sardinia)*

Tyrius, -a, -um, *Tyrian, Phoenician*

U

ubi, adv., *where, when*

ūllus, -a, -um, *any*

umbra, -ae, f., *shadow, darkness*

unda, -ae, f., *wave of the sea*

urbs, urbis, f., *city*

uterque, utraque, utrumque, *each, both*

V

vacuus, -a, -um, *empty*

vallēs, vallis, f., *valley*

vāllum, -ī, n., *rampart, fortification*

-ve, enclitic ending, *or*

veniō, venīre, vēnī, ventum, *to come*

ventus, -ī, m., *wind*

Venus, Veneris, f., *Venus, goddess of love*

vērō, adv., *truly, to be sure*

vestīgium, -iī (ī), n., *track, trace*

vester, -ra, -rum, *your (pl.)*

via, -ae, f., *the way, the road*

vicissim, adv., *in turn*

victor, victōris, m., *conqueror, victor*

videō, vidēre, vīdī, vīsum, *to see*

vinculum, -ī, n., *chain, bond*

violentia, -ae, f., *violence, force*

vincō, vincere, vīcī, victum, *to conquer, overcome; to surpass*

vireō, virēre, viruī, –, *to be green; to flourish*

vir, virī, m., *man, hero*

vīs, vīs (*dat. & abl.*, vī; *acc.*, vim), f., *force, violence, strength*

vīsus, vīsūs, m., *sight, view*

vīvus, -a, -um, *living*

vix, adv., *scarcely, hardly*

vocō, -āre, -āvī, -ātum, *to call*

vōx, vōcis, f., *voice, word*

vulgus, -ī, n., *the common crowd, the masses, the populace*

vultus, vultūs, m., *the face, the appearance*

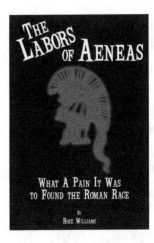

THE LABORS OF AENEAS
What A Pain It Was
to Found the Roman Race
Rose Williams

The Labors of Aeneas is a delightful retelling of Vergil's *Aeneid* that has changed the tone, but not the tale. Ever-faithful to the story's facts, Rose Williams recounts Vergil's epic in a modern's voice—in witty, droll fashion.

Features: • The story of *The Aeneid*, Books I–XII, retold • Black and white illustrations • Notes • A glossary of gods prominent in *The Aeneid*

vi + 108 pp. (2003)
6" x 9" Paperback, ISBN 0-86516-556-4

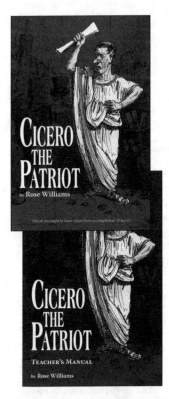

CICERO THE PATRIOT
Rose Williams

Light-hearted in tone but faithful to the facts, this volume interweaves Cicero's private life and feelings with the development of his public life and literary output. Supplementary materials make this an invaluable resource for both students and teachers.

Features: • Complete description of events and historical circumstances of Cicero's life • Timeline of events and publication of Cicero's works • Glossary of terms • One-page summary of Cicero's life

Teacher's Manual Features: • Suggestions for study enrichment • Sample report topics • Further information for the teacher • Thought questions for students • Quick questions to test comprehension

Student: vi + 92 pp. (2004)
6" x 9" Paperback, ISBN 0-86516-587-4

Teacher: xi + 74 pp. (2004)
6" x 9" Paperback, ISBN 0-86516-588-2

BOLCHAZY-CARDUCCI PUBLISHERS, INC.
www.BOLCHAZY.com

A HORACE WORKBOOK
David Murphy & Ronnie Ancona

The Latin text (twenty odes and one satire) that is required reading for the AP* Latin Literature Exam is contained in this workbook along with exercises that will help students practice for the AP* examination on Horace.

A Horace Workbook Teacher's Manual is an excellent resource for both high school and college teachers. Designed to accompany A Horace Workbook (2005), the all-in-one teacher's manual includes the complete student workbook and provides answers directly following each question.

Student Text: xii + 204 pp. (2005) 8½" x 11" Paperback, ISBN 0-86516-574-2
Teacher's Manual: xvi + 273 pp. (2006) 8½" x 11" Paperback, ISBN 0-86516-649-8

A VERGIL WORKBOOK
Katherine Bradley & Barbara Weiden Boyd

The Latin text of Vergil's Aeneid that is required reading for the AP* Latin Literature Exam is contained in this workbook. The exercises in the workbook give students practice with all aspects of the AP* Vergil syllabus: content, translation, meter, grammar, syntax, vocabulary, figures of speech, and literary analysis. In addition, the format of the exercises accustoms the students to all the kinds of questions found on the AP* Vergil Examination. The Teacher's Guide will provide answers and grading guidelines.

Student Text: x + 262 pp. (2006) 8½" x 11" Paperback, ISBN 0-86516-614-5

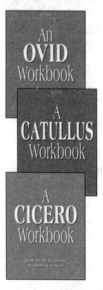

OTHER TITLES IN THIS WORKBOOK SERIES

Like the other volumes in this series, each of these workbooks will contain the Latin text that is on the AP* syllabus accompanied by exercises (grammar, translation, short answer analysis, scansion if appropriate, figures of speech, and essay questions) that will both help students to read and understand the literature as well as prepare for the AP* examination. In addition, teacher's manuals that feature the entire student text along with the answers are planned for each title.

AN OVID WORKBOOK
Charbra Adams Jestin and Phyllis B. Katz
Student Text: (Forthcoming) ISBN 0-86516-625-0
Teacher Manual: (Forthcoming) ISBN 0-86516-626-9

A CATULLUS WORKBOOK
Helena Dettmer and LeaAnn A. Osburn
Student Text: (Forthcoming) ISBN 0-86516-623-4
Teacher Manual: (Forthcoming) ISBN 0-86516-624-2

A CICERO WORKBOOK
Jane Webb Crawford and Judith A. Hayes
(Forthcoming) ISBN 0-86516-643-9

*AP is a registered trademark of the College Entrance Examination Board, which was not involved in the production of, and does not endorse, this product.

BOLCHAZY-CARDUCCI PUBLISHERS, INC.
WWW.BOLCHAZY.COM

VERGIL'S AENEID
Selections from Books 1, 2, 4, 6, 10, and 12, 2nd edition
Barbara Weiden Boyd

This edition is designed for high school Advanced Placement* and college level courses: a newly updated and revised version of selected passages from Vergil's *Aeneid, Books I–VI*, by Clyde Pharr. Passages included are: 1.1–519; 2.1–56; 199–297, 469–566, 735–804; 4.1–448, 642–705; 6.1–211, 450–476, 847–901; 10.420–509; 12.791–842, 887–952.

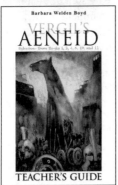

Boyd expertly guides the reader in translating difficult passages, often suggesting two ways to take a given construction. Her interpretive comments are quite helpful in understanding the intricacies of the poem and in providing inspiration for discussion and research projects . . . Boyd's textbook will likely attract a loyal following . . .
– Daniel N. Erickson, *The Classical Outlook*

Student Text: (2004, 2nd edition)
Paperback, ISBN 0-86516-584-X • Hardbound, ISBN 0-86516-583-1
Teacher's Guide: (2002) Paperback, ISBN 0-86516-481-9

VERGIL'S AENEID
Books I & II
Waldo E. Sweet

This unique book features a paraphrase in easy Latin facing the original to help students understand the plain meaning of the author. Instead of a typical Latin-English vocabulary, there are selected notes from Servius and others in Latin, explaining the words and phrases of the original. As a result, this excellent text has been said to offer the student total immersion in Latin.

163 pp. (1960, Reprint 1983) Paperback, ISBN 086516-023-6

*AP is a registered trademark of the College Entrance Examination Board, which was not involved in the production of, and does not endorse, this product.

BOLCHAZY-CARDUCCI PUBLISHERS, INC.
WWW.BOLCHAZY.COM

PARSED VERGIL
Completely Scanned-Parsed
Vergil's *Aeneid* Book I
With Interlinear and Marginal Translations
Archibald A. Maclardy

An irreplaceable, primary resource for educators teaching or reading Book I of the *Aeneid*. The complete text, an interlinear translation, complete metrical scansion, and an accompanying, more polished translation are just part of this goldmine. At the bottom of each page below the text, each Latin word is completely parsed. The commentary includes useful references to the revised grammars of Bennett, Gildersleeve, Allen and Greenough, and Harkness and delves into word derivations and word frequencies.

> . . . teachers, scholars, and non-experts can be confident that they are using the most thoroughly and reliably parsed text of Vergil in existence.
> – Ward W. Briggs, Jr.

iv + 348 pp. (2005, reprint of 1899, 1901 edition) 6" x 9" Paperback, ISBN 0-86516-630-7

VERGIL VOCABULARY CARDS
for AP* Selections
Dennis De Young

A Complete Vocabulary, Grammar, and Poetry Reference for AP and College Vergil Classes*

Four invaluable study aids! This set includes: • 587 vocabulary flashcards, divided into three groups (by frequency of occurrence), on perforated cardstock; full Latin vocabulary entry on one side (with macrons, accents, and complete principal parts for verbs and nominative and genitive forms for nouns), English meanings plus select derivatives/cognates on the other side • full AP* selections vocabulary list • grammatical form summaries, reproduced from *Graphic Latin Grammar* • additional quick-reference guide on Meter, Rhetorical Terms, Figures of Speech, and Rhetorical Devices

250 pp., Perforated cardstock (2005) 8½ " x 11" Paperback, ISBN 0-86516-610-2

*AP is a registered trademark of the College Entrance Examination Board, which was not involved in the production of, and does not endorse, this product.

THE ART OF THE AENEID
2nd edition
William S. Anderson

Anderson's text captures both the toughness and the tenderness of the greatest work of Latin literature. Includes examinations of each book of the *Aeneid*, extensive notes, suggestions for further reading, and a Vergil chronology.

> The classic book for English readers of *The Aeneid*.
> –*American Journal of Philology*

viii + 121 (1969, 2nd edition 2005) Paperback, ISBN 0-86516-598-X

WHY VERGIL?
A Collection of Interpretations
Stephanie Quinn, ed.

43 selections by 38 authors including: • W. H. Auden • Herbert W. Bernario • D. C. Feeney • Robert Frost • Erich S. Gruen • W. R. Johnson • Bernard M. W. Knox • Brooks Otis • Michael C. J. Putnam • Meyer Reinhold • Charles Segal • Marilyn B. Skinner

> Stephanie Quinn's collection should benefit anyone interested in the study and understanding of Vergil, regardless of one's level of expertise in the Vergilian text.
> –Sophia Papaioannou, *Texas Classics in Action*

(2000) Paperback, ISBN 0-86516-418-5
Hardbound, ISBN 0-86516-435-5

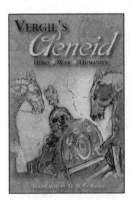

VERGIL'S *AENEID*
Hero • War • Humanity
Translated by G. B. Cobbold

At last the pillar of Western literary tradition is available as a reader-friendly novel that retains the poetic vividness of the original. *Vergil's Aeneid: Hero • War • Humanity* resonates with the challenges of today's world.

This vibrant edition of the *Aeneid* includes sidebar summaries, engaging in-text illustrations, and five indices.

xviii + 366 pp., 91 Illustrations: 12 b&w full-page + 79 b&w in-text; 1 map
(2005) 5" x 7 ¾" Paperback, ISBN 0-86516-596-3

BOLCHAZY-CARDUCCI PUBLISHERS, INC.
WWW.BOLCHAZY.COM

SERVIUS' COMMENTARY
on Book Four of Virgil's *Aeneid*
An Annotated Translation
Christopher M. McDonough, Richard E. Prior,
and Mark Stansbury

Servius' Commentary is important not only as a source of information on Virgil's poem but also for its countless gems about Roman life and literature. Its value has remained unquestioned.

Features: • Frontispiece: Facsimile page from the 1536 edition of Servius' commentary on Book 4 • Introduction on the life of Servius and the textual tradition • Latin text of Virgil's *Aeneid*, Book 4, with Servius' Commentary below • Facing-page English translation of both Virgil and Servius • Endnotes • Guide to further reading

xviii + 170 pp. (2004) 6" x 9" Paperback, ISBN 0-86516-514-9

POET & ARTIST
Imaging the *Aeneid*
Henry V. Bender and David Califf

Book/CD combination that juxtaposes images with the AP* text of Vergil and thought-provoking questions. Encourages students to examine the text more closely and reflect more critically upon it.

Features: • Complete text of all lines on the Vergil AP* syllabus • All of Ogilby's plates on CD rom • Questions in English that require the students to compare and contrast Vergil's Latin text with the illustrations on the CD

xvi + 88 pp. (2004) 8 ½" x 11" Paperback + CD-ROM, ISBN 0-86516-585-8

VERGIL: A LEGAMUS Transitional Reader
Thomas J. Sienkewicz and LeaAnn A. Osburn

11 selections (about 200 lines) from Vergil's *Aeneid*, Books I, II, and IV, designed for students moving from elementary or intermediate Latin into reading authentic Vergilian Latin. Many reading aids, introductory materials, illustrations, and a grammatical appendix.

Features: • Pre- and post-materials help students understand underlying cultural/literary concepts and Vergil's style • Short explanations of grammar/syntax, with exercises • 1st version of Latin text has • gapped words in parentheses • difficult noun-adjective pairings highlighted • complete vocabulary/grammatical notes on facing page • 2nd version of Latin text in its unchanged form has literary notes on facing page • 3 concluding Latin passages with facing-page notes on grammar, vocabulary, and literary analysis, but without transitional aids • Pull-out end vocabulary for unglossed items

xxiv + 136 pp. (2004) 8 ½" x 11" Paperback, ISBN 0-86516-578-5

*AP is a registered trademark of the College Entrance Examination Board, which was not involved in the production of, and does not endorse, this product.

BOLCHAZY-CARDUCCI PUBLISHERS, INC.
WWW.BOLCHAZY.COM

VERGIL'S AENEID: Books I–VI
Clyde Pharr

Both paperback and clothbound now contain an "Annotated Bibliography on Vergil, to Supplement Pharr's *Aeneid*," by Alexander McKay, a bibliography of articles and books in English, for use in college and high school Vergil courses, for students and their teachers.

Illus., xvii + 518 pp. + fold-out (1964, Reprint 1998)
Paperback, ISBN 086516-421-5 • Hardbound, ISBN 086516-433-9

VERGIL'S AENEID 10 & 12
Pallas & Turnus
Barbara Weiden Boyd

Supplements Pharr's *Vergil's AENEID*

Features:

- Contains text for X.420–509 and XII.791–842, 887–952
- Introduction for each section
- Notes and vocabulary on same pages
- Complete vocabulary in back

... For all AP* programs which have been using a text of books 1–6 ... this is unquestionably the ancillary text to use for the revised syllabus. Its excellence guarentees that it will not be so only in default of other options.
— John Higgins, The Gilbert School

The notes are more than scholarly: they are practical. More than once Boyd tells the reader in what word order to "take" a clause or phrase. This kind of information is often a salvation for students—and for teachers, too. ... Anybody can pull lines out of a work, but not everyone can bring the lines alive and make the text work the way Boyd has with the notes. ... This book was a joy to review.
— Gaylan DuBose, Fulmore Middle School and Guardian Angel Academy

No teacher of Vergil should be without this book.
— T. Keith Dix, University of Georgia

Student Text: xii + 44 pp. (1998) Paperback, ISBN 0-86516-415-0
Teacher's Guide: vi + 13 pp. (1998) Paperback, ISBN 0-86516-428-2

FOR MONTHLY SPECIALS VISIT WWW.BOLCHAZY.COM

*AP is a registered trademark of the College Entrance Examination Board, which was not involved in the production of, and does not endorse, this product.

BOLCHAZY-CARDUCCI PUBLISHERS, INC.
WWW.BOLCHAZY.COM

THE LIVING VOICE OF LATIN
Vergil: Selections
read by Robert P. Sonkowsky

Selections from the *Eclogues*, the *Georgics*, and the *Aeneid*.

The readings incorporate the Restored Classical pronunciation of Latin after the scholarly conclusions of historical linguistics and endeavour to interpret the selections in accord with the text.

"Sonkowsky's fine baritone renders selections from *Aeneid* 1, 2, 4, 6, 8, 9, 11 and 12, *Eclogues* 1, 2, and 4, and *Georgics* 4.315–566, totaling three hours.

The 5-page preface surveys his intentions: to demonstrate the restored classical pronunciation (on some distinctive features, of which, like nasalized final "m", he comments); and to assign proper value particularly to both accent and quantity as well as the other audible elements of Vergil's art."

–Edward V. George, *Classical World*

Order #23685: booklet and 2 cassettes

VERGIL'S *DIDO* & *MIMUS MAGICUS*
Composed by Jan Novák; Conducted by Rafael Kubelik
Performed by the Symphony Orchestra of the
Bayerischer Rundfunk; Original record published by audite
Schallplatten, Germany

Composer Jan Novák's haunting choral rendition of Vergil's ancient poetry commences with the voice of Dido the queen, foreshadowing a tragic tale of love and duty. Widely acclaimed in Europe, Novák's *Dido and Mimus Magicus* is now available to American audiences in a CD recording and a 3-language libretto.

Novák, a student of Bohuslav Martinu, was fascinated by the sound and rhythm of Latin poetry. His *Dido* brings the sound and fury of Vergil into the home, the classroom and the symphony hall.

Limited Edition CD (1997) 40-page libretto in Latin, English, and German, ISBN 0-86516-346-4

ROME AND ITALY
Selections from Books 8 & 11 of Vergil's *Aeneid*
Barbara Weiden Boyd

Latin text of 395 lines of the *Aeneid* (608–731: sheild of Aeneas; 11.498–596—introduction to Camilla; 11.664–835—Camilla's heroicism and defeat), with same-page vocabulary and notes. These passages introduce episodes that can only enrich and deepen appreciation for and understanding of Vergil's poetic project. Vergil's description of the scenes on shield presented to the uncomprehending Aeneas, and of the heroism and defeat, through trickery and misplaced desire, of Camilla (deemed "Italy's ornamment," byTurnus), when considered side by side, invite readers to scrutinize the relationship, both strained and intimate, between Italy and Rome, and to shed light on Vergil's complex undrestanding of that relationship. This edition also includes a glossary of rhetorical terms and figures of speech mentioned in the passages, a selected bibliography, and a full vocabulary.

Student Text: (2006), Paperback, ISBN 0-86516-580-7
Teacher's Guide: (2006), Paperback, ISBN 0-86516-581-5